ALCOHOL USE & ABUSE

This new series is designed to meet the growing demand for current, accessible information about the increasingly popular wellness approach to personal health. The result of a collaborative effort by a highly professional writing, editorial, and publishing team, the *Wellness* series consists of 16 volumes, each on a single topic. Each volume in this attractively produced series combines original material with carefully selected readings, relevant statistical data, and illustrations. The series objectives are to increase awareness of the value of a wellness approach to personal health and to help the reader become a more informed consumer of health-related information. Employing a critical thinking approach, each volume includes a variety of assessment tools, discusses basic concepts, suggests key questions, and provides the reader with a list of resources for further exploration.

James K. Jackson	Wellness: AIDS, STD, & Other Communicable Diseases
Richard G. Schlaadt	Wellness: Alcohol Use & Abuse
Richard G. Schlaadt	Wellness: Drugs, Society, & Behavior
Robert E. Kime	Wellness: Environment & Health
Gary Klug & Janice Lettunich	Wellness: Exercise & Physical Fitness
James D. Porterfield & Richard St. Pierre	Wellness: Healthful Aging
Robert E. Kime	Wellness: The Informed Health Consumer
Paula F. Ciesielski	Wellness: Major Chronic Diseases
Robert E. Kime	Wellness: Mental Health
Judith S. Hurley	Wellness: Nutrition & Health
Robert E. Kime	Wellness: Pregnancy, Childbirth, & Parenting
David C. Lawson	Wellness: Safety & Accident Prevention
Randall R. Cottrell	Wellness: Stress Management
Richard G. Schlaadt	Wellness: Tobacco & Health
Randall R. Cottrell	Wellness: Weight Control
Judith S. Hurley & Richard G. Schlaadt	Wellness: The Wellness Life-Style

ALCOHOL USE & ABUSE

Richard G. Schlaadt

WELLNESS

A MODERN LIFE-STYLE LIBRARY

The Dushkin Publishing Group, Inc./Sluice Dock, Guilford, CT 06437

Library of Congress Catalog Card Number: 91–072189
Manufactured in the United States of America
First Edition, First Printing
ISBN: 0-87967-867-4

Library of Congress Cataloging-in-Publication Data

Schlaadt, Richard G., Alcohol Use & Abuse (Wellness)
1. Alcohol. 2. Alcoholism. I. Title. II. Series.
RC565 613.81 91–072189 ISBN 0–87967–867–4

Please see page 143 for credits

The procedures and explanations given in this publication are based on research and consultation with medical and nursing authorities. To the best of our knowledge, these procedures and explanations reflect currently accepted medical practice; nevertheless, they cannot be considered absolute and universal recommendations. For individual application, treatment suggestions must be considered in light of the individual's health, subject to a doctor's specific recommendations. The authors and the publisher disclaim responsibility for any adverse effects resulting directly or indirectly from the suggested procedures, from any undetected errors, or from the reader's misunderstanding of the text.

RICHARD G. SCHLAADT

Richard G. Schlaadt was awarded his doctorate in education from Oregon State University. He has been at the University of Oregon for 24 years, 12 years as the head of the Department of School and Community Health, prior to his current appointment as Director of the University of Oregon Substance Abuse Prevention Program. He has been active in the health education area as an officer in several health organizations and the author of over 50 professional journal articles and 5 textbooks. Dr. Schlaadt sees the *Wellness Series* as the culmination of a career's work.

WELLNESS:
A Modern Life-Style Library

General Editors
Robert E. Kime, Ph.D.
Richard G. Schlaadt, Ed.D.

Authors
Paula F. Ciesielski, M.D.
Randall R. Cottrell, Ed.D.
Judith S. Hurley, M.S., R.D.
James K. Jackson, M.D.
Robert E. Kime, Ph.D.
Gary A. Klug, Ph.D.
David C. Lawson, Ph.D.
Janice Lettunich, M.S.
James D. Porterfield
Richard St. Pierre, Ph.D.
Richard G. Schlaadt, Ed.D.

Developmental Staff
Irving Rockwood, Program Manager
Paula Edelson, Series Editor
Jane Crain, Developmental Editor
Wendy Connal, Administrative Assistant
Jason J. Marchi, Editorial Assistant

Editing Staff
John S. L. Holland, Managing Editor
Elizabeth Jewell, Copy Editor
Diane Barker, Editorial Assistant
Mary L. Strieff, Art Editor
Robert Reynolds, Illustrator

Production and Design Staff
Brenda S. Filley, Production Manager
Whit Vye, Cover Design and Logo
Jeremiah B. Lighter, Text Design
Libra Ann Cusack, Typesetting Supervisor
Charles Vitelli, Designer
Meredith Scheld, Graphics Assistant
Steve Shumaker, Graphics Assistant
Lara M. Johnson, Graphics Assistant
Juliana Arbo, Typesetter
Richard Tietjen, Editorial Systems Analyst

Preface

ALCOHOL HAS PLAYED a prominent role in American social and political history. Alcohol was widely used in colonial America, when consumption levels far exceeded those of today, and it has retained much of its popularity into the present. Although the national experiment with Prohibition in the 1920s caused a decrease in the consumption of alcohol, it certainly did not do away with it altogether. In 1933 Prohibition was repealed, and drinking—along with the problems associated with alcohol abuse—escalated.

There are many reasons for alcohol's long-standing popularity. Perhaps chief among these is its widely recognized value as a social lubricant. For most drinkers, the consumption of alcoholic beverages is a soothing ritual. Used in moderation, alcohol can enhance social encounters and add a small touch of pleasure to everyday life.

As we are increasingly aware, however, alcohol is also a dangerous drug, one with extensive and almost uniformly harmful side effects. Excessive use of alcohol, we now know, takes a heavy toll on the body, with particularly adverse consequences for many vital organs, including the liver, heart, and even the brain. Worse yet, alcohol is a potentially addictive drug. Alcohol consumption can and in too many instances does lead to alcoholism, a dependence on alcohol that causes the sufferer to lose control over his or her ability to stop drinking. The causes of this dependence appear to vary from individual to individual. Some people have a genetic predisposition toward alcoholism, while others succumb for a variety of psychological, emotional, social, or environmental reasons. Alcoholism, it seems, is a disease for which there is no single cause.

What is clear, however, is that alcoholism is extremely costly, not only to the individual but to society as a whole. Alcoholism plays a major role in many of the most significant social problems of our time, including spouse abuse, crime, poverty, and economic productivity. It can and does have fatal consequences. The threat posed by drunk drivers, for instance, is a particularly serious and tragic result of alcohol abuse. For all these reasons, it is imperative that everything possible be done to curb alcohol abuse and provide effective treatment for alcoholism. The costs of not doing so are simply too great to ignore.

Fortunately, there are today many places to which those in need of such assistance can turn. Alcoholics Anonymous is perhaps the best-known source of help, but there are many others, including a broad range of inpatient and outpatient treatment programs employing a variety of approaches. As more is learned about alcoholism, the chances for effective treatment increase. Since alcoholism affects the family, it is often thought of as a family disease, which means that members of the alcoholic's family may need treatment. Children of Alcoholics and Adult Children of Alcoholics are among the organizations that provide help for these groups.

Above all, however, the ultimate responsibility for preventing alcoholism rests with us as individuals. It is we who need to be on the alert for the warning signs of alcoholism, both in ourselves and among our friends and family. And it is we who need in such instances to seek help as soon as possible.

Given the complex nature of the topic, this book should be viewed not as a definitive work, but rather as a place to begin. The central objective of this book is not to make you into an instant expert, but to help you learn to *think critically* about the alcohol-related claims and counterclaims to which all of us are exposed from time to time. Only then will you be able to distinguish alcohol fact from myth, and only then will you be an informed health consumer.

Richard G. Schlaadt
Eugene, Oregon

Contents

FIGURES

TABLES

A Brief History of Alcohol Use and Abuse

CHAPTER 1

HUMANKIND HAS EXPLOITED the mind- and mood-altering properties of beverage alcohol since ancient times. Evidence suggests prehistoric people brewed a primitive beer, and the Old Testament tells us that Noah cultivated grapes to make wine. Through the ages, people have used alcohol in religious rites and rituals, in social celebrations, in their hospitality customs, to accompany a meal, and as a stimulant to conversation and conviviality.

ANTIQUITY AND THE MIDDLE AGES

Although alcohol was not the only **psychoactive** substance used in ancient Asia, Europe, and Africa, it was the most prevalent. Alcohol was probably discovered accidentally; it is produced naturally through the process of **fermentation**. During this process, yeasts feed on the starches and sugars of fruits and grains, and, if the climate and soil are right, yield alcohol and carbon dioxide. [1] Historically, wine- and beer-making probably developed concurrently with agriculture, as human beings first observed the process of fermentation and then refined it.

Both the ancient Egyptians and Persians made wine. One legend has it that a king of Persia stored grapes in a jar he labeled "poison." One of his concubines, attempting suicide, drank from the jar. She was so delighted in the brew that she presented some to the king, who commanded that henceforth all his grapes be allowed to ferment. [2] According to ancient Egyptian mythology, wine was a gift given to humans by the god Osiris. They believed that Osiris was the first to grow grapes from which to make wine and to derive beer from grains. The ancient Greeks first concocted

Psychoactive: Having the potential to alter mood or behavior.

Fermentation: The process by which the sugar and starches present in fruits or other foods are converted into alcohol.

Did You Know That . . .

Scientists have found evidence of wine-making in the fourth millennium B.C., nearly 1,000 years earlier than had been previously documented.

FIGURE 1.1
A Roman Banquet

Source: Culver Pictures.

During the 1st century A.D., the Roman emperors Caligula and Claudius actively encouraged excessive drinking.

mead, an alcoholic liquor made from fermented honey, malt, yeast, spices, and water. As early as the seventh century B.C., the cultivation of grapes for wine-making was central to Greek agriculture. The ancient Greek ethos was one of **temperance**, but the ritual worship of Dionysus, the Greek god of vegetation and wine, consisted of drunken orgies that sometimes even ended in human sacrifice.

During the third century B.C., after the Roman conquest of the ancient Mediterranean world, wine-making gradually became a cornerstone of the Roman economy. Like the ancient Greeks, the Romans began to celebrate their god of wine, Bacchus, through drunken and orgiastic rituals called **Bacchanalia**. The fabric of ancient Roman society, which had placed primary value on the simple and the temperate, was increasingly corrupted by ambition and excess, and moderation gave way to drunkenness. In an effort to reform, in 186 B.C. the Roman senate outlawed the Bacchanalia. However, these rites reemerged during the first century A.D. under the emperors Caligula and Claudius, who actively encouraged the drunken revels of their subjects.

During the first century B.C., when the Roman Empire was at the height of its power, its vineyards were the foundation of the economy. Efforts were made both to increase domestic consumption of wine and to expand its use and manufacture beyond Italy's borders. Rome's empire began to expand throughout Europe, and the conquerors brought with them what were, for that time, advanced techniques for the cultivation of grapes. Soon these methods were in use throughout the British Isles, Spain, France, and Germany. In Rome itself, the problem of alcohol abuse came more and more to resemble the "drug epidemic" of our own age. In fact, some historians believe that alcoholism, along with greed, corruption, and self-indulgence, played no small role in the decline and fall of the Roman Empire.

With the rise of Christianity, Biblical attitudes increasingly influenced both the ritual and the social uses of alcohol. Jesus and his apostles preached temperance, and wine came to represent the blood of Christ in the Eucharistic feast. Although festival drinking accompanied some early Christian rituals, there was nothing on the order of the drunken excess that characterized many Greek and Roman religious customs. Revelrous consumption of wine and beer resurfaced in the Middle Ages. Monks in monasteries cultivated the grapes and made much of the wine, and clergymen and ordinary people drank both wine and beer in copious quantities.

Temperance: Moderation; temperance movements in the United States stressed moderation, or even total abstinence from alcohol.

Bacchanalia: Feasts celebrating Bacchus, the Roman god of wine.

FIGURE 1.2
Alcohol and Religion

Source: Culver Pictures.

Alcohol is a common symbolic feature of many traditional Jewish and Christian rites, as with the sacrament of communion shown here. In comparison with its prominence in many Greek and Roman rituals, however, alcohol has played a relatively modest role in the observance of both Jewish and Christian faiths.

THE INDUSTRIAL ERA

Beer and wine remained prevalent in the seventeenth and early eighteenth centuries in the Western world. Whiskey and gin also gained widespread popularity. Whiskey was probably first manufactured in Scotland around 1500, and it takes its name from the Scottish Gaelic phrase *uisge beatha,* which means "water of life." [3] The Dutch first concocted gin in 1672 by adding juniper berries to Scottish grain alcohol. To the French, this concoction was known as *ginevere;* to the British, it became simply gin.

During England's Industrial Revolution, which began in the early 1700s, many people migrated from the countryside to the cities, principally London. Between 1700 and 1850, England changed from an agricultural to an industrial economy, with harrowing consequences for society as a whole. These consequences included brutalizing urban tenements, extreme poverty for urban workers, inhumane working conditions, and a surge in problem drinking, as well as other manifestations of social unrest. Cheap gin was readily available, and some employers even dispensed it in lieu of wages. In fact, alcohol abuse was so widespread during the early eighteenth century that it has been dubbed "the gin epidemic."

Throughout the rest of Europe, where beer, wine, and distilled spirits were prohibitively expensive, alcoholic excess was a dubious luxury of the upper classes during much of the eighteenth century. During the nineteenth century, however, beverage alcohol became both widely distributed and inexpensive, and alcohol abuse spread throughout the population. Accounts of this period abound with reports of public drunkenness, accidents in the workplace, and hospitalization for the various mental and physical diseases caused by alcohol abuse.

COLONIAL AMERICA

In the United States, the use and abuse of alcohol date back to the colonial era. As in other societies, the colonists relied on alcohol for its medicinal properties, as a social lubricant, and as an integral part of social rites and celebrations. Moderation was the ideal and drunkenness was not tolerated.

Although Americans were introduced to **distilled spirits** during the 1700s, cider was the most widely consumed beverage until the nineteenth century. Made from apples harvested in New York and the New England states, the cider was fermented in

(continued on p. 8)

Distilled spirits: "Hard" liquor; beverages concocted through distillation, a process that consists of converting a liquid mixture into a vapor by heating it, then collecting the components by condensation.

A Nation of Drunkards

Was early nineteenth-century America really a nation of drunkards? Certainly the clergymen who were crusading for temperance thought so, as excerpts from their sermons and addresses attest. These self-appointed moral guardians, convinced that a hearty indulgence in alcohol was commonplace, increasing, and unprecedented, were filled with apprehension, their sermons filled with despair. Intemperance, they warned, was widespread, "too obvious not to be noticed"; "so common, as scarcely to be thought criminal"; "the fashionable vice of the day." They noted, too, that the United States was among the most addicted of nations, that in this respect it had outstripped all Europe, and that "no other people ever indulged, so universally." Even more alarming in their eyes was the fact that this intemperance was spreading "wider and wider"; "like the plague"; "throughout our country"; "with the rapidity and power of a tempest." Not only did they see excessive use as the crying sin of the nation, but they believed it to be "a *growing* evil"; "*still increasing*"; until America "was fast becoming a nation of drunkards."

A similar alarm was voiced by the nation's most prominent statesmen. It was not so much the use of alcohol that worried them—they all drank to some extent—as its excessive use. George Washington, a whiskey distiller himself, thought that distilled spirits were "the ruin of half the workmen in this Country. . . ." John Adams, whose daily breakfast included a tankard of hard cider, asked, " . . . is it not mortifying . . . that we, Americans, should exceed all other . . . people in the world in this degrading, beastly vice of intemperance?" And Thomas Jefferson, inventor of the presidential cocktail party, feared that the use of cheap, raw whiskey was "spreading through the mass of our citizens." In 1821 George Ticknor, a wealthy Boston scholar, warned Jefferson, "If the consumption of spirituous liquors should increase for thirty years to come at the rate it has for thirty years back we should be hardly better than a nation of sots." The Founding Fathers, fearful that the American republic would be destroyed in a flood of alcohol, were anguished and perplexed.

Other observers, more dispassionate but no less articulate, found American drinking habits deplorable. Foreign travellers, for instance, were surprised and shocked at the amount of alcohol they saw consumed. A Swedish visitor, Carl D. Arfwedson, reported a "general addiction to hard drinking," while a visitor from England, Isaac Holmes, noted that intoxication pervaded all social classes. It was not surprising that Basil Hall, a retired Royal Navy Captain hostile to the new nation's democratic ideals, should be "perfectly astonished at the extent of intemperance." But even the sympathetic English reformer, William Cobbett, deplored American tippling. "I almost wished," he wrote, "that there were Boroughmongers here to *tax* these drinkers.". . .

It was the consensus, then, among a wide variety of observers that Americans drank great quantities of alcohol. The beverages they drank were for the most part distilled liquors, commonly known as spirits—whiskey, rum, gin, and brandy. On the average those liquors were 45 percent alcohol, or, in the language of distillers, 90 proof. It was the unrestrained consumption of liquors of such potency that amazed travellers and alarmed so many Americans. And there was cause for alarm. During the first third of the nineteenth century the typical American annually drank more distilled liquor than at any other time in our history. . . .

While men were the heartiest **topers**, women were not faint-hearted abstainers. Little, however, can be learned about either the reputed 100,000 female drunkards or the more numerous women who consumed from one-eighth to one-quarter of the nation's spirituous liquor. The subject received scant attention because it was "too delicate" to be discussed. The ideal of femininity did discourage tippling, for a woman was supposed to show restraint consistent with virtue, prudence consonant with delicacy, and a preference for beverages agreeable to a fragile constitution. The public was not tolerant of women drinking at taverns or groceries, unless they were travellers recovering from a day's arduous journey. Then the ladies might be permitted watered and highly sugared spirituous cordials. . . .

The male drinking cult pervaded all social and occupational groups. A western husbandman tarried at the tavern until drunk; an eastern harvest laborer received daily a half pint or pint of rum; a southern planter was considered temperate enough to belong to the Methodist Church if he restricted his daily intake of alcohol to a quart of peach brandy. A city mechanic went directly from work to the public house where he stayed late and spent his day's wages. Alcohol was such an accepted part of American life that in 1829 the secretary of war estimated that three-quarters of the nation's laborers drank daily at least 4 ounces of distilled spirits. Liquor was so popular that the army dared not bar the recruitment or reenlistment of habitual drunkards. If such a policy were adopted, warned the surgeon general, the army might have to be disbanded. The middle classes were scarcely more sober. Attorneys disputed with physicians as to which profession was the more besotted. Even more shocking was the indulgence of clergymen. One minister who considered himself temperate systematically downed 4 glasses of spirits to help him endure the fatigues of Sunday. At Andover Seminary, one of the most important centers of temperance activity, students regularly drank brandy toddies at the local tavern. Perhaps this practice was necessary to prepare would-be ministers for keeping up with their future congregations. . . .

Most liquor was drunk in the home, where whiskey and rum provided mealtime drinks, customary refresheners, and hospitable treats for guests. Fashionable people owned ornate liquor cases or elaborate sideboards that contained numerous bottles of various cordials, including mild, sweet, fruit-flavored elixirs for the ladies. Even the poorest host proffered his whiskey jug. While some of this liquor was made on the premises, bartered from neighbors, or bought at a distillery, much came from the general store, where its sale was often the most important item of business. Although some merchants curried favor with their customers by plying them with free samples of their spirits, less liquor was given away than was sold for home use. A study of one New Hampshire store's records from 1810 to 1833 showed that farmers who purchased supplies usually bought liquor along with their other purchases. During the early 1820s one-quarter of the value of this store's total sales was alcohol; typically, at that time, in a transaction that was for more than $1 and that included the sale of alcohol, distilled beverages accounted for more than half the value of the sale. A decade later less than one-tenth of the value of total sales was liquor; in a transaction over $1 that included alcohol, spirits were but one-third the value of the sale.

Leaving home, however, did not require that an American forgo his favorite beverage. When journeying by stage coach, travellers could obtain liquor at the inns where the horses were changed. During one arduous seventeen-hour, sixty-six mile trip across Virginia, the stage stopped ten times, and two of the passengers had drinks at each way station: ten drinks apiece. Such habits led one foreign observer to conclude that "the American stage coach stops every five miles to water the horses, and *brandy the gentlemen!*" With the invention of steamboats, Americans were provided with yet another place to drink. Whereas stage travellers had been able to imbibe only when their vehicle rested at a wayside inn, boat passengers usually found a bar conveniently situated in the gentlemen's compartment, on the middle deck above the engine room. This arrangement is telling. The location of the bar not only discouraged female travellers from drinking; it also indicates that the bar was the boat's central feature. Of all forms of public transportation, only the steamboat focused so much attention on the bar. In part, this design reflected the owners' hopes for high profits from liquor sales; some boats were little more than floating saloons. More important is the fact that the steamboat was conceived at a time when drinking was central to American society. Boat designs that stressed bars conformed to a cultural imperative.

Americans drank not only any place but also

any time. Some began to imbibe even before breakfast with an eye opener concocted of rum, whiskey, or gin mixed with bitters. In one Rhode Island factory town, laborers going to work made their way through the dawn's early light to the tavern "to take a little drop." Gentlemen adjourned from business at 11:00 A.M. for the old-fashioned equivalent of the coffee break, the 'elevens,' an occasion for partaking of spirituous liquor. When the weather was cold, they might have hot toddies made of whiskey or rum, sugar, and hot water, or hot slings made of gin, sugar, and hot water. At times a little lemon juice, cherry brandy, or bitters was added. The Virginia gentry gathered at 1:00 P.M., an hour before dinner, for the purpose of taking juleps compounded of peach brandy or whiskey, sugar, and ice. Sometimes crushed mint was added to make a mint julep. Throughout America early afternoon dinner was accompanied by hard cider or distilled spirits mixed with water; in late afternoon came another break; then supper with more refreshment. Finally, in the evening it was time to pause and reflect upon the day's events while sitting by the home or tavern fireside sipping spirits.

Americans drank on all occasions. Every social event demanded a drink. When southerners served barbecue, they roasted hogs and provided "plenty of whiskey." Guests at urban dances and balls were often intoxicated; so were spectators at frontier horse races. Western newlyweds were customarily presented with a bottle of whiskey to be drunk before bedding down for the night. Liquor also entered into money-making and business affairs. When a bargain was negotiated or a contract signed, it was sealed with a drink; auctioneers passed a whiskey bottle to those who made bids. After the harvest, farmers held agricultural fairs that ended with dinners laced with dozens of toasts. Whiskey accompanied traditional communal activities such as house-raisings, huskings, land clearings, and reaping. It was even served when women gathered to sew, quilt, or pick the seeds out of cotton. . . .

Alcohol was pervasive in American society; it crossed regional, sexual, racial, and class lines. Americans drank at home and abroad, alone and together, at work and at play, in fun and in earnest. They drank from the crack of dawn to the crack of dawn. At nights taverns were filled with boisterous, mirth-making tipplers. Americans drank before meals, with meals, and after meals. They drank while working in the fields and while travelling across half a continent. They drank in their youth, and, if they lived long enough, in their old age. They drank at formal events, such as weddings, ministerial ordinations, and wakes, and on no occasion—by the fireside of an evening, on a hot afternoon, when the mood called. From sophisticated Andover to frontier Illinois, from Ohio to Georgia, in lumbercamps and on satin settees, in log taverns and at fashionable New York hotels, the American greeting was, "Come, Sir, take a dram first." Seldom was it refused.

Early nineteenth-century America may not have been 'a nation of drunkards,' but Americans were certainly enjoying a spectacular binge.

Source: W. J. Korabaugh, *The Alcoholic Republic* (New York: Oxford University Press, 1979), pp. 5–21.

wooden barrels to produce a mild apple wine. This beverage was a dietary staple, taken at every meal and sipped like water throughout the day. Moreover, cider was as integral to socializing as beer or wine is today.

The Slave Trade and Industrialization

During the 1600s, American colonists began to trade with the West Indies, importing sugarcane and molasses, from which they were able to produce domestic rum. Some of this rum was traded

FIGURE 1.3
Annual Consumption of Alcohol per Capita, in the United States, 1720–1970

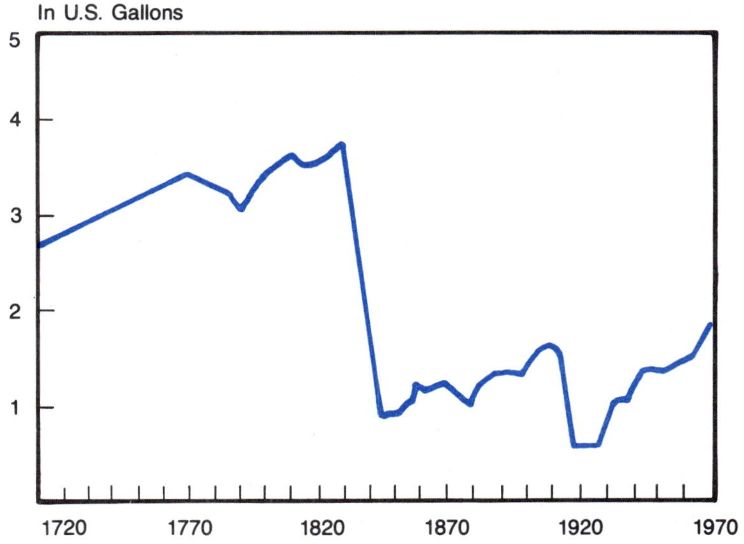

Source: *Journal of Studies on Alcohol*, No. 37 (1976), pp. 360–361.

This chart of alcohol consumption in the United States between 1720 and 1970 shows that rates of drinking in the nineteenth century were twice as high as they are near the end of the twentieth century (see Figure 6.5 on page 112).

for West African slaves, who were then traded back to the West Indians for more molasses. Dubbed "the Triangle Trade," this three-point arrangement had by the mid-eighteenth century become an important part of the commercial life of the American colonies. Woodrow Wilson once remarked, "Out of the cheap molasses of the French Islands, New England made the rum which was the chief source of her wealth." [4]

As community life in the colonies became less cohesive and structured, the social sanctions that had kept drunkenness to a minimum began to lose their power. In fact, some historians tend to mark the Revolutionary War era as a turning point in America's relationship with alcohol, citing it as the time during which widespread moderate use of alcohol began to give way to excess and abuse. [5] During and after the Revolution, the Puritan strictures that had largely determined behavioral norms during the colonial era broke down, and excessive drinking, previously censored, began to be tolerated. [6] By the end of the eighteenth century, alcohol abuse pervaded American society—by 1790, annual alcohol consumption was approximately 6 gallons of pure alcohol per capita, more than twice the current level. [7]

THE TEMPERANCE MOVEMENT

Not surprisingly, the temperance movement in the United States dates back to this turning point in America's drinking habits. On one front, clerics and other guardians of society's morals began to preach with increasing urgency on the immorality of alcoholic excess. On another front, a few isolated medical professionals, most significantly Benjamin Rush and Thomas Trotter (see chapter 5), were just beginning to recognize alcoholism as a disease rather than as a sign of personal weakness.

America's Protestant churches spearheaded the temperance movement. In 1812, the General Assembly of the Presbyterian Church and the General Conference of the Methodist Episcopal Church addressed themselves to the growing problem of alcohol abuse and urged their clergy to speak out against it. The Presbyterian Assembly called for widespread preaching against "the sin and mischief of intemperate drinking." [8]

As the ideal of temperance became a common subject for sermons within organized religions, the movement began to spread like wildfire in rural areas. [9] Thousands of local voluntary associations sprang up during the early nineteenth century, and temperance reform took on the trappings of a genuine religious revival. The aim was to bring political pressure to bear on the problem of **alcoholism**, and the temperance message was broadcast in a blizzard of cheap temperance pamphlets. By 1855, the temperance stalwarts numbered more than 1 million men, women, and children.

Initially, the fervor of the temperance crusaders did result in a radical decline in alcohol consumption and in the passage at the state level of a flurry of laws—most of which were revoked shortly after their enactment—aimed at curbing public drunkenness rather than private use of alcohol. By the 1860s, however, the consumption of beer was on the rise again, and the settlement of the "wild west" after the Civil War was notoriously replete with tales of violent drunken brawls that often ended in crippling

Alcoholism: A disorder characterized by habitual and excessive drinking of alcoholic beverages. It impairs daily social functioning, job performance, and physical health.

FIGURE 1.4
The Home of the Intemperate

Source: Bettmann Archive.

Heavy drinking became more common during the nineteenth century when inexpensive alcoholic beverages became widely available. Alcohol was blamed by some for 90 percent of the misery of the working class.

Did You Know That . . .

The average adult in America currently drinks about 2.5 gallons of pure alcohol each year, as compared to 6.5 gallons per person in 1800.

injury or death. In fact, alcoholism was rampant on the western frontier and contributed in large measure to its lawlessness, harshness, and brutality.

Women played a leading role in the temperance movement. In 1874, the Women's Christian Temperance Union (WCTU) was founded and proclaimed by one of its first presidents as "of the women, by the women, but for humanity." [10] The WCTU became the largest women's association in nineteenth-century America. Its membership consisted mostly of genteel, middle-class women who sought to close down saloons all over the country through peaceful protests and prayer. One notorious exception, however, was Carry Nation. The WCTU's most controversial member, she used violent tactics and often wielded an ax in her efforts to close down saloons in Kansas.

(continued on p. 15)

The Western Frontier and the Rise of the Saloon

While the Far West was not America's first frontier, nor its last, it certainly has been its most celebrated. And no scene epitomizes our image of the Old West more than the Rocky Mountain saloon, where men and women of the frontier gambled, fought, loved and drank. The steely six-gun, the faithful steed, and a shot glass of straight whiskey are symbols of the frontier spirit. How valid is the image that the West was won with a bottle and a six-gun? Did the miner and the cowboy differ from their Eastern counterparts primarily in the prodigious amounts of liquor they could hold?

The Western frontier was a remarkable epoch in the history of American drinking patterns. Abundant supplies of cheap whiskey and the proclivity of itinerant adventurers and drifters to abuse alcohol helped to give the "Wild West" its singular identity. The violence and lawlessness associated with drinking sprees seemed to confirm the worst fantasies of the most inventive Temperance reformers. The legendary saloon, Western counterpart of the grog shop, played a crucial central role in frontier social life until the final phases of the Western expansion. The American West of popular mythology developed from the experience of thousands of men and women who were drawn to California, Colorado, Arizona, New Mexico, Montana and Idaho in search of precious metals. The Western mining frontier lasted roughly half a century, beginning with the discovery of gold in California in 1848. Its history is told in the ledgers of towns such as Tombstone, Arizona, Leadville, Colorado, and Cripple Creek, Colorado. Following the end of the Civil War these towns attracted hordes of prospectors, miners, cardsharks and soldiers of fortune, all of whom demonstrated a strong taste for alcohol. . . .

As immigration to the Western territories accelerated, one institution came to epitomize the lifestyle of the frontier: the saloon. The term saloon is derived from the French *salon,* which was initially used in England and America to describe public meeting places or entertainment halls. By the end of the nineteenth century, its connotation had changed as the Colonial inns and taverns were replaced by a very different type of drinking establishment. Although the saloon was modeled initially after its Eastern counterpart, it quickly adapted to the social needs and drinking styles of the frontier. Indeed, the evolution of the Western saloon closely parallels the economic and social development of the Western town from frontier camp to rural community. As the central forum for Western drinking, its development helped to structure the very drinking style it was intended to serve.

The first saloons were typically rudimentary structures, often consisting of a tent or a shack with a row of barrels for a bar. Like the wood frame structures of the frontier camp itself, the saloon could be cheaply constructed with minimal investment. When decoration was added it often reflected a style best described as "Victorian macho," typified by paintings of naked women, pictures of boxer John L. Sullivan or illustrations of Custer's Last Stand. Such decorations mirrored the characteristics and aspirations of the saloon's patrons: male dominance, aggressive bravado, and the tendency to exploit both men and nature. The emerging image of the saloon was also reflected in the descriptive names that gave each a special identity. Names such as the Miner's Rest, the Pioneer, the Big Tent Saloon, or the Dew Drop Inn, often were associated with the most typical clientele, some characteristic of the structure or with the owner's sense of humor. . . .

The Western saloon became the frontier's most versatile social institution. It served a variety of important needs that were critical to the growth and development of the West. Just as the New England tavern served as a forum for Colonial commerce and politics, so the Western saloon became a focal center of frontier society. In the absence of town halls and other public buildings, the saloon was often the seat of the county court, the site of the first post office, and host to public ceremonies. It was the meeting place where business deals were negotiated, and a recruitment center for laborers and volunteers. At the early stages of a town's development, it was the major clearinghouse for rumors, news and job-related information. Inasmuch as the saloon always contained a significant cross section of the town's population, its potential as a public meeting place was quickly recognized by churchless ministers in search of a congregation, frontier politicians in search of votes, and itinerant entertainers in search of an audience.

But the most important function of the saloon was to provide diversion, entertainment and refreshment. In addition to the standard games such as poker, billiards and checkers, the saloon frequently sponsored special activities like dances, lotteries, competitions, contests and prizefights. These entertainments were designed to attract large crowds and served as a focal activity around which drinking could be organized and prolonged, to the obvious delight of the saloonkeeper.

The convergence of large numbers of ambitious, unmarried male adventure seekers on the Western frontier created the kind of social disorder long celebrated in legend and film. Consistent with the image of the raucous and bawdy frontier settlement, historians of the period have noted that much of the brawling and killing was associated with drinking. Newspaper accounts suggest, for example, that one or both parties were drinking heavily in at least half of the fourteen murder incidents occurring in Leadville between March and October, 1880. In Silverton and Georgetown, Colorado, 60 percent of the misdemeanor arrests in the early years were for public intoxication. Among the most vexatious problems to the public authorities were barroom brawls, robbery, drunken assaults, the shooting of handguns in the air, rowdy behavior near saloons, and intoxicated patrons riding wildly through town. Another problem, frequently noted by the frontier physicians, was alcohol-related death from pneumonia and exposure. Cold winters and inhospitable terrain took a steady toll of the malnourished, chronically intoxicated "losers" who failed to find their fortunes in the West.

Thus by all accounts the explosive drinking style that emerged on the Western frontier conformed rather closely to the negative stereotype popularized in the "Temperance Tales" of the Prohibitionists. Four factors seem to have been paramount in the development of this drinking pattern. The first is the ready availability of cheap intoxicants. Because of the relative ease of transport, cheap whiskey was often the only beverage that could be hauled long distances over rugged terrain. For the same reasons that distillation proved to be so profitable in the East, teamsters and saloonkeepers in the West found that selling alcohol to the thirsty hordes of arriving immigrants was a sure way to make a profit. Frontier whiskey often consisted of raw alcohol mixed with water, and its wretched quality is reflected in such names as "extract of scorpions," "San Juan paralyzer" and "Taos Lightning." The latter was a wheat whiskey first distilled in New Mexico for fur traders and later adopted by the Southwestern miners.

By the early 1870s, beer became more popular than whiskey in the West as well as the East. Technological improvements like bottling and pasteurization led to the development of major regional brewers such as Schlitz, Pabst, Blatz and Budweiser. Many of the more successful Midwestern German brewers constructed mountain breweries in the larger and more established Western towns, which could then supply the local markets. Improved transportation also made possible the direct shipment of beer from the giant breweries of St. Louis and Milwaukee. By the 1880s most Westerners enjoyed a dependable and varied supply of local and regional beers.

A second determinant of the Western drinking style was the demand created by mobile men who were far from the moderating influences of family and community. In the mining camps especially, group drinking assumed ritualistic and symbolic functions as a facilitator of conviviality, solidarity and information exchange. Census reports reveal that approximately 50 percent of the early Western immigrants were American born, and the remainder were recent immigrants from Europe, Mexico and Asia. Of the Europeans, English, Irish and Germans accounted for the largest ethnic blocks. Men outnumbered women in the early days of most settlements by a factor of five to one. Because the Western frontier attracted a particular type of individual, these demographic statistics convey only a part of the picture of the Western immigrant. Men who were unemployed, unemployable, rootless and alienated were particularly attracted to the West, and their itinerant life-style placed them at risk for the development of drinking problems.

Yet another ingredient that contributed to the typical Western drinking pattern was the nature of work and leisure on the frontier. Work on the trail or in the mines was monotonous. Winters were long and imposed further isolation on those already separated from family and friends. Lack of entertainment and organized social activity increased the importance of communal drinking as a pastime, particularly following long periods of relative abstinence. Under these circumstances whiskey and a warm saloon became a welcome center of social life. Drinking for relief from drudgery and escape from worries was an accepted pattern. Thus, the cyclical contrast between long periods of hard, dangerous work and brief periods of intense recreation was common to the life-style of the cowboy and the miner, the northern lumberjack and the Far West trapper, the seaman whaler and the clipper ship merchant. To those whose work did not impose involuntary abstinence, these "blowouts" could assume a commonplace regularity. One Colorado editor observed that "It is a custom of the boys to 'irrigate' to a considerable extent, when they strike a bonanza. Some of them strike one every day."

Under these circumstances drinking became associated with almost all aspects of work and leisure in the West. Stage drivers, mule packers and wagon train guides often drank during their long journeys. Certain holidays, especially Christmas, Independence Day, and St. Patrick's Day, became occasions for drinking to intoxication for want of alternatives. The practice of treating, where one person buys a round of drinks with the expectation that all the other drinkers will eventually reciprocate, was especially conducive to heavy drinking.

A final feature that contributed to the development of the Western drinking style was the lack of social controls on the frontier. Not only were there no constraints on the marketing and production of alcoholic beverages, there were not enough peace officers to control legal offenders. In many towns, the saloon flourished even after the passage of statewide prohibition, because local legal authorities were not strong enough to confront the unruly mobs of drinkers or the strong economic interests that catered to them.

As the heterogeneous, transient nature of Western settlement gave way to a more organized management of economic and social development, other businesses and institutions gradually assumed the functions of the saloon. With the growth of public services and facilities, and the emergence of a more permanent work force, the image and the functions of the saloon began to change. Land and opportunity attracted men with families, and families had a far greater commitment to community development and long-range economic interests than their more adventuresome predecessors. Gradually, drinking establishments began to reflect the new social realities. Barrooms tended to become specialized around the needs of a particular clientele; some catered to political clubs, others to the town's business elite, still others to the predominant ethnic or occupational group. At the same time, the more successful saloons took on the appearance of permanence and refinement. Establishments like Tombstone's Crystal Palace, which graced the main streets of the more prosperous Western towns, were often more elaborately designed and furnished than the local church or the town hall. Undoubtedly the imported accoutrements, expensive fixtures, fine stemware and luxurious furniture added an aura of bourgeois respectability to drinking, as did the introduction of music and dancing. But the majority of saloons remained rather dingy enclaves serving a predominantly male clientele.

The arrival of a new type of settler, immigrants and native-born Americans less concerned with instant wealth, did not directly threaten the existence of the saloon at first. However, the values and social outlook of these more stable settlers contrasted sharply with the sordid traditions of the hard-drinking frontier subculture. The clear association between drinking and disorder invited criticism from the new middle class and the older, more established, citizens. The inevitable result of midnight revelers shooting their pistols in the air or drunken brawls and homicides was increased concern with control of the liquor trade. These solid citizens were a ready source of sympathy and support for the Temperance organizations that developed in the Western territories and newly-admitted states.

Source: Jack H. Mendelson and Nancy K. Mello, *Alcohol: Use and Abuse in America* (Boston: Little, Brown & Co., 1985), pp. 49–55.

Drinking patterns in nineteenth-century America were closely related to the drinking habits of the immigrants who arrived in successive waves during that time. Rightly or wrongly, stereotypes became attached to the various ethnic groups that composed the increasingly urbanized and industrialized society: total abstinence became associated with middle-class Protestant respectability, whiskey drinking with the Irish, beer consumption with the Germans, and wine with the Italians. [11]

During the 1880s and 1890s a second wave of temperance laws was passed throughout the country, although these statutes, like those that had been passed during the mid-nineteenth century, were quickly repealed, liberalized, or unenforced. But nationwide pressure for complete prohibition continued to mount and was brought to bear on lawmakers by the Protestant churches, temperance organizations, and the Prohibition Party, which was formed in 1869 expressly to work for laws that would outlaw the manufacture and sale of alcoholic beverages.

Founded in 1803, the Anti-Saloon League campaigned fiercely for prohibition at the state level between 1906 and 1913. By 1912 complete prohibition was in effect in 7 states; in a number of other states prohibition failed to pass by only the smallest of margins. In 1917, with two-thirds of the states having ratified the **Prohibition** Amendment, it was submitted to the U.S. Congress, which ratified it as the Eighteenth Amendment on January 29, 1919. Prohibition went into effect a year later. Meanwhile, on October 28, 1919, the National Prohibition Act, commonly known as the **Volstead Act** after the congressman who championed it, was enacted; it outlined policies for the enforcement of Prohibition.

The Eighteenth Amendment prohibited the manufacture, importation, exportation, transportation, and sale of alcoholic beverages in the United States and its possessions. The amendment did not, however, outlaw the purchase or use of these beverages. Although Prohibition did reduce the consumption of

Prohibition: The U.S. Constitution's Eighteenth Amendment, enacted in 1919 and repealed in 1932; it outlawed the sale of liquor in the United States.

Volstead Act: The congressional act that outlined the policies for Prohibition.

FIGURE 1.5
Carry Nation's Crusade

Source: Culver Pictures.

"I cannot tell a lie—I did it with my little hatchet!" Carry Nation was a notorious member of the temperance movement who used violence and theatrics to influence public opinion.

alcohol nationwide, particularly in rural areas and small towns, it was largely ineffective as a corrective to alcoholism. [12] Disregard for the law was rampant in the nation's cities, and enforcement throughout the 1920s was erratic. [13] Moreover, vast criminal fortunes were amassed through the illegal manufacture, sale, and importation of alcoholic beverages. Historians estimate that Al Capone, the notorious Chicago **bootlegger**, earned approximately $60,000,000 a year ruthlessly presiding over a violent empire maintained through gang warfare and murder.

Bootlegger: A person smuggling liquor from foreign countries or selling it illegally in the United States.

As the 1920s wore on, disenchantment with Prohibition intensified. In 1932, the Democratic Party called for repeal of the Eighteenth Amendment in its presidential platform; the party's victory that year virtually assured the demise of Prohibition. In February 1933, Congress adopted a resolution calling for a Twenty-first Amendment to the Constitution to repeal the Eigh-

(continued on p. 18)

Woman has always drunk, sometimes surreptitiously, sometimes openly. But no matter how she has chosen to indulge, she has not had an easy time of it in our dual-standard society, especially if she drinks too much. The history of women and alcohol has been tempestuous: In early times women were scorned for drinking like men; in more recent days they took up the banner of temperance; presently, women drink with men but are still subject to disparaging attitudes.

Women and Drink

In ancient Rome, philosopher/statesman Seneca declared caustically, "In rivalling male indulgences, [women] have also rivalled the ills to which men are heirs. They keep just as late hours, and drink just as much liquor; . . . they devise the most impossible varieties of unchastity, and in the company of men they play the part of men. . . . Because of their vices, women have ceased to deserve the privileges of their sex." The literature of that period contains allusions to laws that actually prohibited women from drinking, tales of husbands killing wives who violated those laws, and reports of women forced to kiss their male relatives to prove their lips had not touched wine. Pliny the Elder mentioned a woman who was starved to death because she stole the keys to a wine cellar.

In more recent times, Prohibition saw a similar distinction between drinking men and women. "There has always been a theory that it was possible to 'drink like a gentleman,' " observed one social commentator of the period, Margaret Culkin Banning. "Deplored though his habits might be by the more temperate, a gentleman could reach the point of complete intoxication and yet not lose his standing. Large claims have even been made that a man best shows his real nature when he is drunk. But until recently no such claim has ever been made for a lady nor similar facts admitted of her. If she drank past the point of mental and physical control, she no longer was a lady. Be her previous station high or low, she was an unfortunate creature indisputably on the down grade."

On the other side of the spectrum emerged the image of woman as the fiery, hatchet-wielding foe of drink. Those in the forefront of the American Temperance Movement were strong-willed women who often had drunken, abusive husbands and who, although their attitudes were understandable, warped the true meaning of temperance—"moderation in action, thought, and feeling"—so that it came to mean total abstinence. The anti-salooners like Carry Nation, who at the turn of the century wrecked many a barroom in Medicine Lodge, Kansas with her hatchet, did much to strengthen the ideal (or the myth) of women as foes of alcohol and guardians of morality.

This image of women shunning drink, however, quickly disappeared during Prohibition as virtually everyone—the public, law enforcement officials, even President Harding (who kept a well-stocked bar in the White House)—openly flaunted the restrictive Volstead Act that legislated the shift from wet to dry. There was plenty of alcohol, whether home-brewed beer, moonshine liquor, bathtub gin, or "the real stuff," supplied by organized crime and bootleggers. Much of this contraband was dispensed in speakeasies, local cabarets or taverns operating in an atmosphere of false secrecy (given the fact that police surveillance was quite relaxed) that catered to both men and women.

The 1920s drinking scene was aptly described by American social historian Frederick Lewis Allen: "Father may still go down to Cassidy's bar of evenings, but since prohibition mother goes down with him. Under the new regime not only the drinks were mixed, but the company as well. . . . Among well-to-do people the serving of cocktails before dinner became almost socially obligatory. Mixed parties swarmed up the curtained grilles of speakeasies and uttered the mystic password. [Women] along with men stood at the speakeasy bar with one foot on the old brass rail. The late afternoon cocktail party became a new American institution."

And with it all came a revolution in morals and manners and a new view of drinking that included women, a view that may well have left its mark on humankind for better or for worse. The drinking woman had burst upon the scene.

Source: John Langone and Delores de Nobrega Langone, *Women Who Drink* (Reading, MA: Addison-Wesley Publishing, 1980), pp. 1–3.

teenth. On December 5, 1933, Utah became the thirty-sixth state to ratify the Amendment, and the "noble experiment," as Prohibition has sometimes been called, came to an end.

With the repeal of Prohibition, control of the manufacture and sale of alcoholic beverages was returned to the states. Some states controlled the manufacture, sale, and distribution directly; others relied on a licensing system that enabled them to control the ways in which manufacturers, wholesalers, and retailers did business. The goal of both approaches was to promote public health and welfare by regulating the flow of alcohol. The economic depression of the 1930s, coupled with the high cost of beverage alcohol, kept the rate of consumption well below pre-Prohibition levels until after World War II.

THE "AGE OF ENLIGHTENMENT"

Most prohibitionist sentiment had been fueled by a moralistic revulsion against drunkenness and a system of values that was anti-urban, anti-ethnic, and focused on the virtues of discipline, family, and frugality. Although there had been some pioneering work done during the nineteenth century on the medical and psychological plight of the alcoholic himself, by and large this research was disdained or ignored by the establishment, and the public viewed alcoholism as a depravity rather than a disease.

In 1935, an event took place that was to revolutionize not only the medical community's attitude toward alcoholism but the treatment of the disease as well. That year a New York City stockbroker named Bill Wilson, who had been on the downward spiral of heavy drinking for years, had what he described as a transforming spiritual experience. He came to believe that the only way he could stay sober permanently was by helping other alcoholics achieve sobriety as well. Through a series of circumstances he found himself at the bedside of Dr. Bob Smith, an Ohio physician who had been hospitalized for medical emergencies caused by his own alcoholic drinking. Together, the two men founded **Alcoholics Anonymous (AA)** and went on to help thousands of other alcoholics recover through a program that relied on spiritual principles and the compassionate understanding of fellow sufferers. Most important, the early success of AA demonstrated to a skeptical public that, once sober, alcoholics were not hopeless degenerates after all, but decent and productive human beings.

After the founding of Alcoholics Anonymous, alcoholism came more and more to be viewed as a treatable disease. Finally, in 1958, the American Medical Association recognized the **disease theory of alcoholism**. Increasingly, both the health-care and the scientific communities have come to accept this theory, although controversy still rages over whether alcoholism is primarily a physical or **psychological** disorder. Those who hold that it is a physical disorder theorize that it may be **genetically** or **physiologically** based. The psychologists see it as a symptom of emotional imbalance. There are also differing viewpoints about how it can be treated most effectively. [14]

Nonetheless, despite the lack of unanimity on what the cause of alcoholism actually is, we have indeed come a long way from both the colonial era, when "drunkards" were beaten and pilloried, and from the hatchet-wielding self-righteousness of Carry Nation. Today public policy is geared more toward education and prevention than censure and punishment. Sophisticated research into the nature and causes of alcoholism is widespread, and there is a proliferation of treatment programs and professionals available to those alcoholics who seek help. Although the stigma has by no means been lifted entirely, a new commitment to understand and treat this ancient malady has ushered in an era of hope for its millions of victims and their families.

Alcoholics Anonymous (AA): A voluntary organization founded in 1935, consisting of individuals seeking help for a drinking problem. The AA program is based on total abstinence, achieved by following a 12-step process.

Disease theory of alcoholism: A theory of alcoholism endorsed by Alcoholics Anonymous and others, in which alcoholism is seen as a disease rather than a character defect or social failing.

Psychological: Relating to the mind.

Genetically: Pertaining to heredity; of or involving genes.

Physiologically: Pertaining to bodily functions.

CHAPTER 2

Alcohol and the Body

UNTIL THE LATE 1960s, alcohol was regarded not as a drug, but as a kind of food. To be sure, alcohol is rich in calories, and the body's **cells** can use the quick energy alcohol provides to perform their complicated functions. However, unlike other foods, alcohol has almost no vitamins and minerals and contributes nothing to the body's nutritional needs. Although the deleterious effects of alcohol on the mind and body have been well documented for centuries, the downside of abusive drinking was always ascribed not to the excessive consumption of alcohol in itself but rather to a poor diet, personal habits, and living conditions. During the late 1960s, Charles Lieber, a researcher at the Mount Sinai School of Medicine in New York City, demonstrated in animal experiments on baboons that alcohol alone causes the physical damage associated with alcoholism. [1]

Cell: The basic structural unit of living organisms, consisting of an exterior wall or membrane, a nucleus, cytoplasm, and other structures.

Ethanol: The colorless, volatile form of alcohol that is the active ingredient in alcoholic beverages; also known as ethyl alcohol or grain alcohol.

Distillation: A process in which liquids are heated to the boiling point to convert them to a gaseous state, after which the resulting vapors are cooled (condensed), making it possible to collect certain components of the original liquid, e.g., alcohol, in more concentrated form.

WHAT IS BEVERAGE ALCOHOL?

The chemical name for the form of alcohol found in beverages is ethyl alcohol or **ethanol**. The manufacture of alcoholic beverages involves two separate processes: fermentation and **distillation**. Fermentation is a biological process in which yeasts are used to change carbohydrates, such as sugars and starches, into alcohol. Distillation is a physical process by which alcohol produced by fermentation is concentrated and made more potent by the removal of water. All alcoholic beverages are fermented; beer and wine are not distilled, but stronger beverages, such as whiskey, vodka, gin, rum, and brandy are.

(continued on p. 23)

Is All Alcohol Equal?

"A drink is a drink, no matter what you drink." Or so says the House of Seagram. But ask the top three television networks who refused to air this "public service" message, or the brewing and wine industries, and you may get a different response. The message is the theme of Seagram's $10 million "equivalency" advertising campaign, which states: "12 ounces of beer, 5 ounces of wine and 1¹/₄ ounces of liquor all have the same alcohol content." Opponents of the ad claim the message is not only self-serving but misleading. In refutation, the Winegrowers of California released a statement that cited research on the evils of distilled spirits and the boons of wine.

If this leaves you confused about drinking wine or the hard stuff, perhaps consider beer. A recent study done at the Johns Hopkins School of Medicine for the Alcoholic Beverage Medical Research Foundation (ABMRF)—which is funded by U.S. and Canadian brewers—found that moderate beer drinkers appeared healthier than nondrinkers or drinkers of wine or liquor, reporting illness 13 percent less often than expected.

These reports and messages have stirred things into a muddle as murky as a black russian. Essential questions are unanswered: Is it actually better or worse to drink any one type of alcohol? Is it better to drink at all? And how much can the conflicting findings espoused by the various industries be trusted?

The National Institute of Alcohol and Alcohol Abuse (NIAAA), part of the Department of Health and Human Services, has some answers. "We do not dispute the equivalence message," says Kenneth Warren, acting director of the institute's Office of Scientific Affairs. In fact, the NIAAA has pushed this message for over 16 years. Warren says, "We're concerned that even today many wine and beer drinkers think they're consuming beverages that are less alcoholic." Seagram, citing a recent survey that shows significantly more people judge wine, beer and distilled spirits to be equal both in alcohol content and in effect, claims its ad campaign is turning the tide.

The alcohol in all alcoholic beverages is ethanol. In the body, ethanol gets absorbed through the small intestine and goes directly to the liver, where it is metabolized by the enzyme alcohol dehydrogenase. But, explains Warren, "alcohol dehydrogenase gets saturated quickly." This means that if a lot of ethanol enters the liver, only part is metabolized. The rest continues into the blood.

Warren emphasizes that it is the blood alcohol content (BAC) that

Did You Know That . . .

Drinking different types of alcohol, such as beer, wine, and hard liquor, during the same evening will not make you drunk any faster than drinking just one kind of alcoholic beverage.

causes impairment. And, he says, "the main influence on BAC is how fast ethanol is absorbed from the intestine. This doesn't depend on what you drink but on how fast the alcohol leaves the stomach, and this, in turn, depends on how fast you are drinking and how full you are."

The Winegrowers of California reached different conclusions when it reviewed past studies on the subject. Among its findings: Wine delays the rate at which alcohol leaves the stomach, and distilled spirits consumed while fasting result in a 33 to 130 percent higher peak BAC.

Warren is skeptical of these studies, many of which are over 40 years old: "There are questions as to experimental accuracy and appropriate statistical treatment of the data. On the basis of papers published, I don't believe the winegrowers can validly make such conclusions."

There is another side to the equivalency argument: the social and behavioral aspects of alcohol consumption. Some studies have found that beer is implicated in most drunk driving incidents. And because most wine is consumed with meals, it is absorbed more slowly.

Alex Richman, who headed the study, is a psychiatric epidemiologist at Dalhousie University in Nova Scotia and chairman of the ABMRF's Behavioral and Social Advisory Council. He is quick to point out the importance of psychosocial parameters in his research. The reason beer drinkers reported being more healthy, he says, is probably "related to **life-style.** Beer drinkers may be more sociable and convivial. They may be more concerned with moderation in general."

That moderate drinking promotes health, especially a reduced risk of heart disease, is not a novel theory. A probable mechanism involves increased levels of HDL cholesterol, the "good" cholesterol that scavenges artery-clogging LDL cholesterol. But, adds Warren, this mechanism is true for all alcoholic beverages.

Robert Pandina, scientific director of Rutgers University's Center of Alcohol Studies, warns of sloppy **correlational studies.** He asks, "Do healthier people choose to drink beer or are they healthier because of the beer they drink?" He also questions studies that compare the health of moderate drinkers and nondrinkers: "Most nondrinkers don't drink because of sickness or religious conviction or because they are recovering alcoholics. Relatively few people just choose not to drink. In this light the message that you are healthier because you are a moderate drinker becomes questionable."

In the scientific community, the real questions pertain to the psychosocial aspects of drinking: what type of person tends to drink how much of what, when, and to what end. But all agree on one point: If you frequently drink a significant quantity of any type of alcohol, risks of all sorts increase.

Source: *Science Digest,* May 1986, p. 17.

Life-style: A style of living that consistently reflects a particular set of values and attitudes.

Correlational studies: Studies in which the researcher attempts to measure the extent to which one or more variables or characteristics are associated (correlated) with one or more other variables or characteristics.

BLOOD ALCOHOL CONCENTRATION

Absorption of alcohol into the bloodstream begins through the **epithelium**, or lining, of the mouth. About 20 percent of any alcohol consumed passes immediately from the stomach into the bloodstream. The remaining 80 percent passes through the small intestine and then into the blood. Once it is in the bloodstream, alcohol is quickly diffused throughout the body and enters most body cells through passive **diffusion**. Alcohol is water soluble and therefore reaches its greatest concentration in those body organs that naturally contain a large amount of water.

To determine the concentration of alcohol in the body at any given time, it is necessary to establish the **blood alcohol concentration** (BAC), which measures the percentage of alcohol in the blood. When a person consumes more alcohol than his or her body can immediately eliminate (the body eliminates alcohol at the rate of approximately one-half ounce of absolute alcohol per hour), alcohol accumulates in the bloodstream and the BAC rises. One-half ounce of absolute alcohol is roughly the amount contained in a 12-ounce can of 4 percent beer, a 4-ounce glass of 12

FIGURE 2.1
Alcohol Molecule

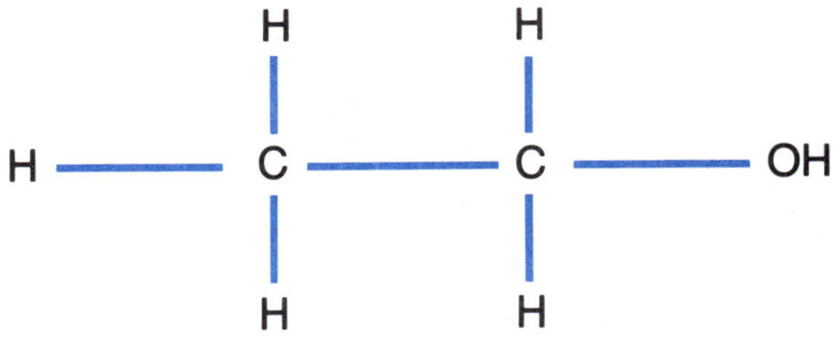

C—Carbon Atom
H—Hydrogen Atom
OH—Hydroxyl Group

This figure shows how the elements of carbon, oxygen, and hydrogen are combined to form an alcohol molecule. The hydroxyl group (OH) is formed by joining one hydrogen atom to one oxygen atom. Water (H_2O) also contains a hydroxyl group. Because hydroxyl groups are attracted to each other, alcohol and water mix easily. As a result, alcohol can travel throughout the body wherever water is present.

Epithelium: One or more of the cellular layers that completely cover the surface of the body, including the interior cavities and passages.

Diffusion: A process through which the molecules of one substance intermingle with the molecules of another substance.

Blood alcohol concentration (BAC): The percentage of alcohol found in the bloodstream; it is used to determine levels of intoxication.

FIGURE 2.2
Alcohol Levels in Different Drinks

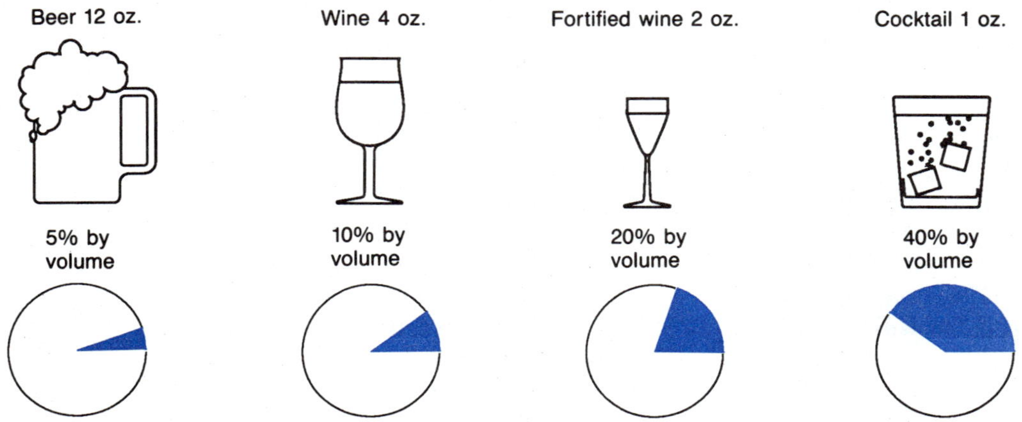

Alcoholic drinks come in many forms, as shown here. Although the percentage of alcohol by volume varies among these drinks, the drinks each contain approximately equal amounts of pure alcohol.

Did You Know That . . .

At 1 to 1,000 parts of alcohol-to-blood (a level of .10 percent), walking and talking are affected. At blood alcohol levels of .30 to .40 percent, the drinker goes into a coma.

percent wine, or a 1.25-ounce serving, or "shot," of a 40 percent distilled spirit such as whiskey.

As Figure 2.3 illustrates, alcohol's effects are progressively more noticeable as the blood alcohol concentration increases. At a BAC of .02 to .05 percent, the effects are almost entirely pleasurable. The drinker feels relaxed and sociable. There may also be some modest impairment of reasoning or memory and a general reduction in caution. The overall effect, however, is one of *euphoria.* Alcohol is not alone in its ability to induce such feelings. However, its capacity to do so quickly combined with its social acceptability goes a long way toward explaining its popularity.

A BAC of .05 to .08 percent produces a state of *excitement.* The drinker begins to suffer from what may be a slight but nonetheless noticeable impairment of balance, speech, vision, reaction time, and hearing. Judgment and self-control are also affected. The drinker's behavior is apt to become more aggressive. In general, the drinker feels stimulated and highly capable. In reality, his or her ability to safely perform tasks such as driving that require quick reactions, concentration, and good judgment has been significantly reduced.

(continued on p. 26)

FIGURE 2.3
Blood Alcohol Concentration (BAC)

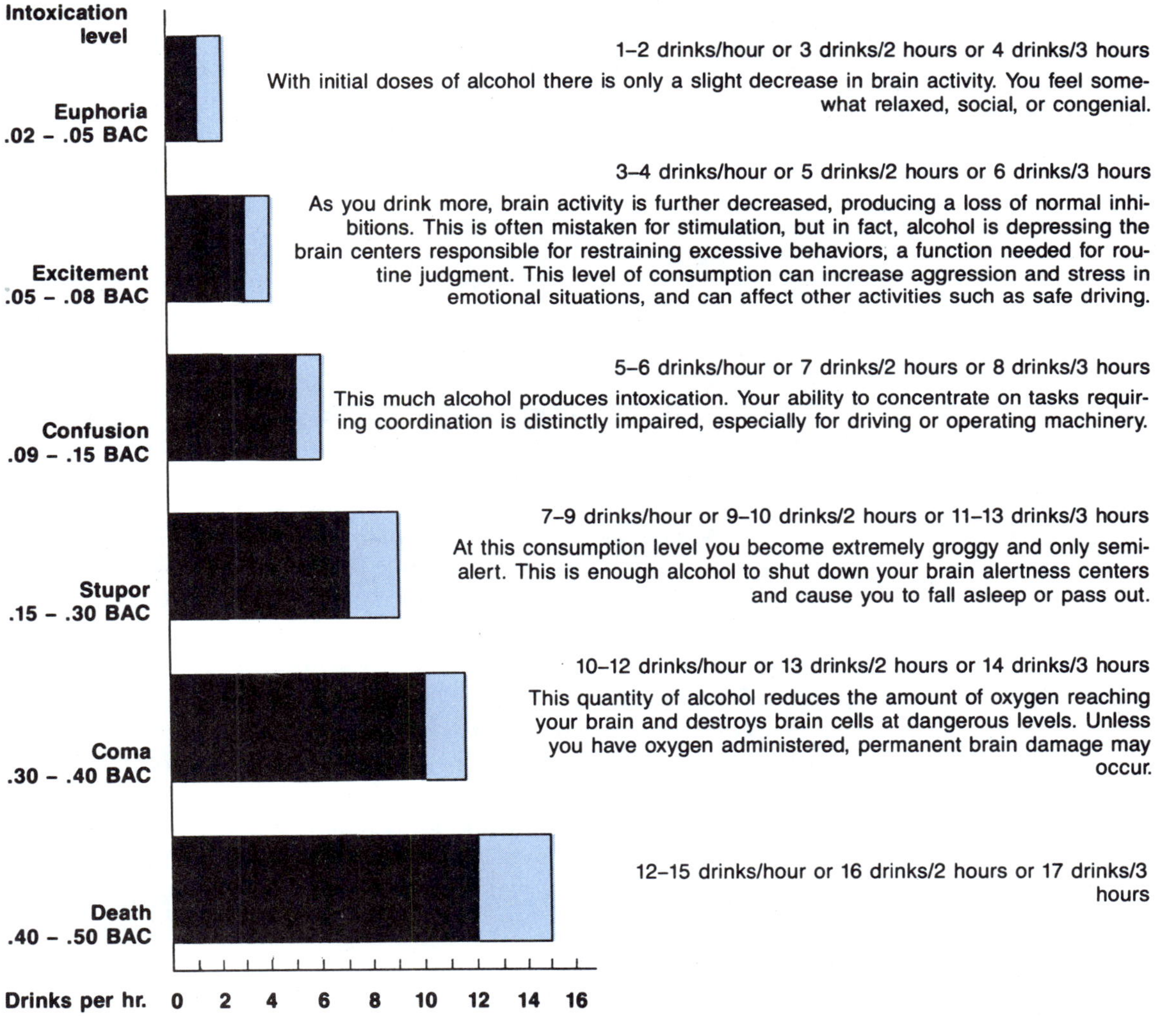

Source: Adapted from *Using Alcohol Responsibly*, Drug Information Center (Eugene, OR: University of Oregon, 1985), p. 5.

A healthy person can break down, or oxidize, approximately one drink per hour. The progression of effects depicted here is calculated for a 150-pound male. However, the effects of a given level of consumption will vary (sometimes significantly) with individual differences such as weight, sex, drinking on an empty stomach, and so on. Because alcohol appears to have a greater effect on women than on men, women (and men who weigh less than 150 pounds) may find that even one drink per hour produces a greater level of intoxication than shown here. If so, they should monitor and adjust their consumption accordingly.

Did You Know That . . .

It takes approximately as many hours to sober up as the number of drinks ingested. For example, a person who drinks 2 drinks will take about 2 hours to become sober.

A drinker's ability to function deteriorates quickly at BACs in excess of .08. At a BAC of between .09 and .15 percent, the drinker enters a state of *confusion.* This is the level at which one becomes legally intoxicated in most states, with a BAC of .10 percent being the most common legal definition of **intoxication** at the present time. By this stage, the level of impairment becomes obvious, if it has not already. Speech becomes slurred; the drinker's sense of balance, vision, reaction time, hearing, and reasoning ability are distinctly and obviously impaired. Drinkers whose BAC is .09 percent or above cannot safely perform tasks that require sound judgment or motor coordination. They should, among other things, never operate a motor vehicle. The difficulty, of course, is that someone who has reached this level of intoxication may refuse to believe his or her abilities are in any way impaired. Too often, the results of such misplaced confidence are tragic.

BACs above .15 percent have a progressively severe and obvious effect. Starting at a BAC of approximately .15 percent, the brain's alertness center begins to shut down. By the time the BAC reaches .30 percent, the drinker is in a *stupor.* He or she is almost certain to fall asleep or pass out.

BACs above .30 percent are potentially life threatening. At a BAC somewhere between .30 and .40 percent, the drinker falls into a *coma,* which may or may not result in irreversible brain damage. A BAC above .40 percent almost invariably results in death, usually because of respiratory failure. [2]

The rate at which the blood alcohol level rises differs from drinker to drinker and is determined by a number of factors. One of these is weight: The more a drinker weighs, the more water there is in the body to dilute the alcohol and therefore the lower the BAC will be. For example, a 200-pound man might have a BAC of approximately 0.15 percent after drinking 8 cans of beer, whereas a 150-pound male drinking at the same rate might have a 0.20 percent BAC after drinking the same amount. Naturally, the drinker with the higher BAC would act more intoxicated. Thus, it is the BAC and not the amount of alcohol consumed that determines alcohol's effects on behavior. [3]

Another factor that influences the BAC is gender. Observers have long noted that women tend to "handle" alcohol less efficiently than men, typically showing signs of intoxication more quickly and at a lower level of alcohol intake than men. [4] There are at least three possible explanations. The first has to do with the fact that any alcohol which cannot be immediately processed and eliminated by the liver goes into solution throughout the

Intoxication: A state in which one's ability to function is clearly and significantly impaired as a result of the consumption of alcohol or other intoxicating substance.

body. Since, on average, a woman's body contains less water than a man's in which to dilute the alcohol, this has the effect of raising the alcohol concentration in the blood (and in other bodily fluids). So does the fact that women's bodies contain more fat than men's, since alcohol does not easily penetrate fatty tissue. Finally, **hormones** also seem to affect BAC. Researchers have found, for example, differences in the BAC of women who were tested at different points in their menstrual cycle after consuming the same quantity of alcohol. These women's BAC levels were consistently higher premenstrually and lower on the first day of their cycle.

In the January 11, 1990, edition of the *New England Journal of Medicine,* a team of researchers advanced another theory that might help explain women's greater vulnerability to alcohol. Although their findings are quite complex, they first state that a more significant amount of alcohol than was previously thought is metabolized in the gastrointestinal system through the action of an **enzyme** called **alcohol dehydrogenase (ADH)** before diffusing into the bloodstream. [5] Prior to this study, it was believed that alcohol dehydrogenase worked primarily in the liver. Second, they report that the amount of alcohol metabolized by ADH is lower in women than in men. Third, the study concludes that the gastric **metabolism** of alcohol is decreased in women and men with **chronic alcoholism**. In other words, in women and in chronic alcoholics, the essential work of alcohol dehyrogenase is retarded, and more pure alcohol is delivered into their bloodstreams than is the case with men and nonalcoholics. Thus, women will have higher BACs, given a consumption of alcohol equal to men's. Furthermore, the degree to which a chronic alcoholic's gastric metabolism is impaired is greater for female alcoholics than for male alcoholics—that is, women become even less able to metabolize alcohol. This study, which received a great deal of publicity when it was first published, raises crucial questions on the physiological nature of alcoholism and opens up exciting new avenues of inquiry. [6]

The amount of food in a drinker's stomach also has a significant effect on BAC. When the stomach is empty, there is no food to absorb even part of any alcohol consumed or to slow down its absorption into the bloodstream. Consequently, the BACs of those who drink on an empty stomach rise more rapidly than the BACs of those who eat something before or while they are drinking. Conversely, food in the stomach, particularly food rich in carbohydrates, tends to slow the rate of absorption of alcohol into the blood.

(continued on p. 29)

Hormone: Any of the chemical substances secreted by glands in the body that are released directly into the bloodstream and elicit specific responses from a targeted organ, muscle, or other structure.

Enzyme: A protein that can cause chemical changes in other substances without being changed itself.

Alcohol dehydrogenase (ADH): An enzyme naturally present throughout the body that helps metabolize alcohol, primarily in the liver and stomach.

Metabolism: The physical and chemical process whereby the body transforms food into energy by breaking large molecules into smaller molecules.

Chronic alcoholism: Alcoholism that persists over an extended period of time.

Alcohol and Women

Alcohol does not affect everyone the same, and that is particularly true with women. In fact, one drink for a woman may have the same effect as two drinks for a man.

Scientists have found that women become drunk more quickly than men because their stomachs are less able to neutralize alcohol.

As a result, the researchers say, much more alcohol goes directly into the bloodstream through the stomach wall. From there it goes to the brain, making the women drunk, and to the liver, causing more damage.

The finding is even more pronounced among alcoholic women, because the stomach apparently stops digesting alcohol at all, the researchers say. On the other hand, alcoholic men are still able to digest some of the alcohol they consume.

The research, prepared by scientists in the United States and Italy, was reported in the *New England Journal of Medicine.*

The findings may explain why women often say they feel the effects of alcohol more than men, even if they consume the same amount of alcohol relative to body size.

It may also explain the well-documented observation that women are more susceptible than men to liver damage when they become alcoholics.

In the report, Dr. Charles Lieber of New York's Mt. Sinai School of Medicine and his colleagues said that much of the alcohol that people drink is broken down by an enzyme in the stomach and never reaches the bloodstream.

However, women have less of the stomach enzyme than men do, so more of what they drink enters the bloodstream in the form of pure alcohol.

The researchers said they do not know why women have less of the enzyme.

In general, the researchers found, women get about 30 percent more alcohol into the blood than men of similar weight who drink the same amount.

And, considering that men are generally bigger than women, Dr. Lieber said, the findings mean that one drink for a woman has the same effect as two for a man.

"There is no question that if a woman takes two drinks, her level of impairment will be greater than a man who takes two drinks, even if she is exactly the same size (body weight) as a man," Dr. Lieber said.

He and his colleagues have also found that the stomach enzyme works less well when people drink heavily. Alcoholic men lose some ability to digest alcohol, and alcoholic women have essentially no working enzyme, the researchers said.

"For them, drinking alcohol has the same effect as injecting it intravenously," Dr. Lieber said.

Drinking on an empty stomach puts even more alcohol into the bloodstream. "Fasting accelerates the emptying of the stomach, so the alcohol does not have time to be metabolized," he said.

In addition, the popular ulcer drug cimetidine, or Tagamet, makes the stomach enzyme less active, doubling the blood alcohol levels of alcohol in men who take the drug and drink, compared with men who do not take the drug.

Dr. Lieber says he has not yet studied the effect of Tagamet in women but suspects they are similar. "A person who is not eating and who is taking Tagamet is in real trouble," he said.

Other experts on alcohol metabolism and alcoholism said they were intrigued by the new results.

"I think it's fascinating," said Dr. Steven Schenker, an alcoholism researcher at the University of Texas who wrote an editorial accompanying Dr. Lieber's paper. "It's an exciting piece of work by a very highly respected group."

The enzyme in question was long known to be present throughout the body, Dr. Lieber said, but it was felt that it did not play a significant role in alcohol metabolism.

The reason was that when researchers tested the enzyme with levels of alcohol like the levels found in the blood after drinking, it was inactive.

Only the alcohol dehydrogenase in the liver breaks down alcohol at those concentrations, so it was assumed that the liver is the sole organ which metabolized alcohol.

But Dr. Lieber reasoned that when people drink, they end up with enormously high concentrations of alcohol in the stomach, much higher than the amount of alcohol in the blood. So, he said, "We tested the stomach enzyme at very high concentrations of alcohol," concentrations like those found in the stomach when people were drinking. He found that the enzyme metabolized the alcohol.

Working first with rats and then with men, Dr. Lieber found that the stomach enzyme normally metabolizes about 20 percent of the alcohol that is drunk, preventing it from getting to the bloodstream.

He said that explained what had been a puzzling experimental finding. People have higher blood levels of alcohol when the substance is injected into the blood than they have when they drink the same amount of alcohol.

But all the studies had been with men. Researchers had previously found that women have more alcohol in the blood than men have when they drink equivalent amounts, but the researchers attributed it to the fact that women have more body fat and proportionately less water in body tissues than men do. With a smaller amount of alcohol the drink would be diluted by the body's water, the researchers theorized.

But the problem is that the water effect "is relatively negligible," according to Dr. Lieber.

In the study reported in the *New England Journal,* Dr. Lieber decided to assess the activity of the stomach enzyme in women. He and his colleagues compared 20 men and 23 women. Six of each group were alcoholics.

In the study, the researchers gave the volunteers three-tenths of a gram of alcohol per kilogram of body weight, an amount equivalent to one or two drinks.

In terms of the study, a drink was defined as a 12 ounce glass of beer, a 5 ounce glass of wine, or an ounce and a half of 86 proof alcohol.

Source: *The Bottom Line on Alcohol in Society,* Vol. 9, No. 3 (Lansing, MI: Alcohol Research Information Service, 1990), pp. 34–36.

The rate at which alcohol is absorbed into the bloodstream is also affected by whatever mixer might be used with the alcohol. Mixing alcohol with water or fruit juices slows down the rate of absorption. Carbonated mixers, such as tonic or club soda, tend to speed up the process.

ALCOHOL AND THE BRAIN

As we have said, the alcohol **molecule** easily penetrates most bodily tissues. Within minutes of entering the bloodstream, alcohol finds its way into every organ of the body, including the brain, liver, heart, pancreas, lungs, and kidneys.

To understand how alcohol affects the brain at a cellular and biochemical level, we need a basic knowledge of how individual brain cells transmit messages to one another. The brain has two major kinds of cells: **neurons** and **glia**. About 85 percent of brain

Molecule: The smallest unit of a substance that exhibits all of the substance's properties and is capable of independent existence; molecules ordinarily consist of 2 or more atoms joined together.

Neurons: Impulse-conducting cells that are the functioning units of the nervous system.

Glia: Cells in the central nervous system that regulate the chemical environment of the nerve cells. RNA is stored in glial cells.

Spinal cord: A tubular cord of nerve tissue that is surrounded by the vertebrae and serves as the primary channel for sensory and motor messages between the brain and the rest of the body.

Nucleus: A sac-like structure found in all living cells that contains the cell's genetic material.

Cytoplasm: A jelly-like substance found in all plant and animal cells that is contained by the cells's external layer (membrane), and within which the cell nucleus is suspended.

Axon: A tail-like filament that projects from the body of a nerve cell (neuron) along which nerve impulses (signals) are conducted between the nerve cell and other neurons or tissue.

Dendrites: Any of the branching protoplasmic structures of a nerve cell that receive impulses from other nearby cells.

Synapse: The juncture between neurons.

Neurotransmitters: The chemical messengers that convey messages from one neuron to another.

Receptor: A specific molecule in a neural cell that receives messages from a neighboring neuron.

Gamma-aminobutyric acid (GABA): A neurotransmitter that scientists believe regulates anxiety in the brain.

cells are glia, which are responsible for guiding the brain's development and for removing waste products. But it is the neurons that are responsible for controlling the body's essential activities and for giving human beings their capacity to think and tactilely sense.

Neurons are nerve cells, and those in the brain are essentially the same as the other neurons that run down to form the **spinal cord** and fan out to every part of the body. Like all other cells, neurons have a main cell body consisting of a **nucleus** surrounded by **cytoplasm**. Unlike other cells, neurons have long extensions, up to 4 feet long, called **axons**. Axons are the links that allow messages to pass from one neuron to another. Axons make contact with shorter extensions on neighboring cells called **dendrites**. A single neuron can have many axons and more than 10,000 dendrites, each capable of receiving signals from many other neurons.

A nerve cell is separated from its neighbor by a narrow gap called a **synapse**. Nerve cells communicate with one another via chemical messengers called **neurotransmitters**. Sometimes a neurotransmitter causes a neighboring nerve to send an impulse. Sometimes it prevents a neighboring nerve from sending an impulse. A neurotransmitter from one nerve cell acts on the neighboring cell by attaching itself to a specific molecule in that cell's membrane. That molecule is called a **receptor**. Each receptor recognizes only one neurotransmitter. Think of the way a key fits into a lock to understand the way in which each specific neurotransmitter attaches to its designated receptor. Once a neurotransmitter has acted on its specific receptor, it is deactivated in one of several ways. Some neurotransmitters are destroyed by enzymes, but most are taken up by the neuron that released them in the first place.

All drugs, including alcohol, influence this highly complex and specific pattern of brain activity. Some drugs interfere with it by preventing the formation of neurotransmitters. Others cause neurotransmitters to leak out of nerve cells. Still others increase the activities of neurotransmitters, either by undermining the enzymes designed to destroy them or by preventing their recapture by the neuron that released them. Most commonly, however, drugs disrupt neurotransmitter functions by actually mimicking the neurotransmitter itself, competing with the neurotransmitter by fitting into its receptor site.

Normally, a neurotransmitter called **gamma-aminobutyric acid (GABA)** regulates anxiety in the brain. Researchers have very recently discovered that alcohol strongly affects areas of the

(continued on p. 32)

FIGURE 2.4
The Synapse Connection

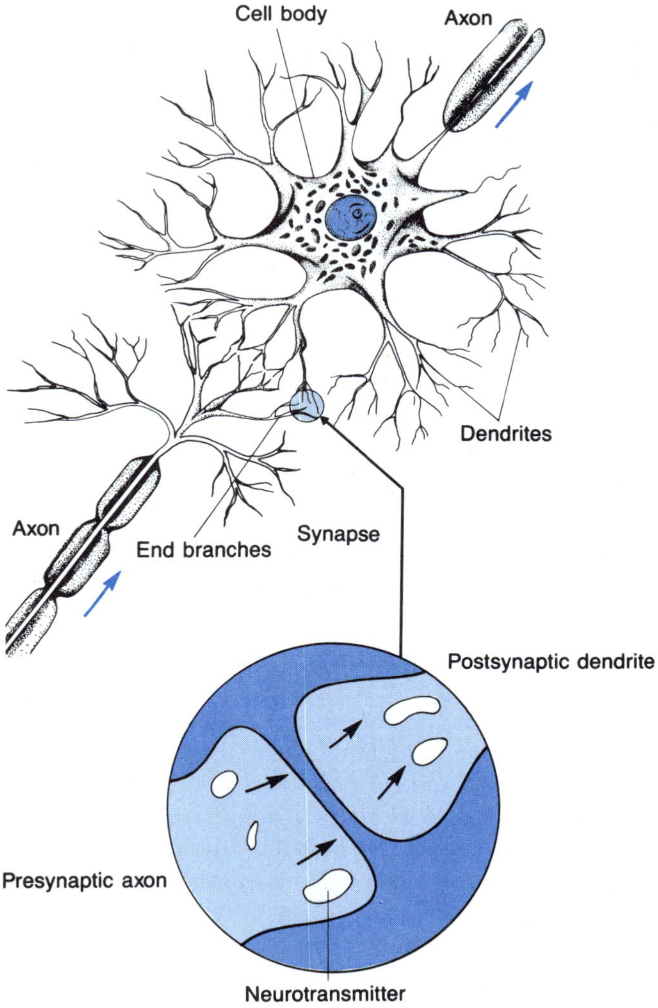

The synapse is the space between the axon of one neuron and the dendrites of the next. When the electrical neural impulse reaches the end of the axon, it releases a chemical neurotransmitter into the synapse. This crosses the synapse and causes the dendrites of the next neuron to fire. When alcohol is consumed, this highly complex activity is disrupted.

brain with high concentrations of GABA receptors, including the **cerebellum**, which controls motor coordination; the **hippocampus**, which is responsible for information retrieval; and the **cerebral cortex**, where **cognitive** processes take place.

Serotonin is another neurotransmitter whose functioning may be negatively influenced by alcohol. It is known that excessive aggression is related to serotonin deficiencies, and researchers have begun to speculate that these deficiencies may be related to alcoholism. [7] **Acetylcholine** and **somatostatin-14** are two other neurotransmitters that are significantly affected by intoxicating doses of alcohol. In experiments on laboratory animals, alcohol has been shown to have a strong influence on the working of these brain chemicals in the hippocampus, a structure deep within the brain that plays an important role in learning and memory. [8] Although findings are not conclusive yet, it is reasonable to speculate that changes in the hippocampus caused by drunkenness are responsible for the memory lapses and "blackouts" (a total inability to recall events even though the person does not lose consciousness and may appear to be functioning normally while drunk) some heavy drinkers experience. [9]

Normally, the brain is protected from chemicals and drugs by an electrical-chemical filter system called "the blood/brain barrier," which screens out all but the most simple molecules, such as those of oxygen and water. Because of its relatively simple molecular structure, alcohol passes right through this protective screen into the brain and its extension, the spinal cord.

Alcohol's easy access to the brain accounts for its immediate and profound effects on behavior. We have seen that these effects progress as the blood alcohol level (BAC) rises. This is because alcohol penetrates and influences first one part of the brain and then another, with consequent disruptions of each area's proper functioning. At low doses, alcohol seems to act as a stimulant to the brain; this is because even small amounts of alcohol weaken the control exercised by the higher brain centers. After one or two drinks, the drinker is apt to feel relaxed, talkative, and carefree. This is primarily because the alcohol is already at work on a part of the brain called the **reticular activating system**, which controls the flow of information from all the sensory organs to the cerebral cortex, the center of higher thought processes.

As the BAC rises, other parts of the brain are increasingly affected. At a BAC of 0.2 percent, the part of the brain that controls motor activity is significantly depressed, and the drinker is apt to be staggering and uncoordinated, assuming he or she can still stand up at all. Speech is slurred and vision impaired.

(continued on p. 34)

Cerebellum: The part of the brain responsible for muscle and movement control, and coordination of eye and body movement.

Hippocampus: One of several structures in the central part of the brain that comprise the limbic system; the hippocampus plays an important role in memory processing.

Cerebral cortex: The part of the brain in which thought and memory processes take place.

Cognitive: Pertaining to thought and memory.

Serotonin: A neurotransmitter, produced in the brain stem, that is involved in sleep and sensory experiences.

Acetylcholine: A neurotransmitter involved in the activation of muscle movement, memory, motivation, and arousal.

Somatostatin-14: A neurotransmitter, produced in the brain and pancreas, that helps regulate the production of insulin.

Reticular activating system: Scattered groups of nerve cells located in the brain stem that collectively screen and regulate the flow of sensory information to the brain; also known as the reticular formation.

Alcohol's Effects

Alcohol's Path in the Body

Alcohol is a speedy and deliberate drug. Unlike most drugs that enter the body only from the intestines, alcohol slips in from the entire gastrointestinal tract—from the stomach, the bowels, the inside of the mouth. It will even enter through the skin.

Alcohol doesn't hang around in the stomach waiting to be digested but zips through the body just as it comes from the bottle. Put a thimbleful of alcohol on the tongue, and seven seconds later you can find traces in the arm. That's essentially the speed of blood circulation.

Alcohol invades cell membranes throughout the body and alters normal cell activity (just how is not yet wholly understood). Because it mixes totally with water, alcohol concentrates in the body's wetlands—the blood, the liver, and especially of concern in drunk driving, the brain.

In the brain, alcohol first attacks the higher mental functions, things like judgment and prudence and attention. As more alcohol is consumed, it penetrates more layers, impairing such things as coordination and the ability to recite the alphabet. Finally, it affects basic motor functions—consciousness, heartbeat, respiration. . . .

Factors Affecting Body's Response to Alcohol

Although alcohol already consumed cannot be counteracted, something counteractive can be done before or during consumption. Eating. Especially eating something like potatoes or bread that soaks up liquor. Alcohol in the grip of French fries is slowed on its race through the body, giving the system more time to dispose of it.

The body rids itself of alcohol in two ways, metabolism and excretion. Despite frequent calls of nature during drinking bouts, 90 percent of alcohol in the body is disposed of by metabolism. The liver is the principal organ of alcohol metabolism and does its work at a rate of less than an ounce of whiskey, or a 12 ounce beer, an hour.

That rate of metabolism yields a formula for safety: drink no more than one drink an hour, and your body will burn up the problem. Be aware, however, that the path into and out of drunkenness is a crooked one, different for each person.

One important variable is weight. If all other functions are equal, which they never are, a 200-pound person should be able to drink twice as much as a 100-pound person and show similar effects. The heavier the person, the more room the alcohol has to spread out. If, however, a 150-pound man and 150-pound woman drink equal amounts (all else being equal), the woman will get drunker faster. That's because she has relatively more fatty tissue than he does and a smaller pool of body fluid in which the alcohol can mix.

The time of day can be a factor. Some people can drink at dinner with little effect, but a beer at lunch puts them to sleep. Some people have a stronger will than others to resist the effects of drink, while the person who invites the effects of alcohol is more likely to receive them. A healthy person will be less affected than someone in poor health.

Alcohol Combined with Other Drugs

Some medications—antihistamines and tranquilizers are common examples—act with alcohol to produce effects that are additive (equal to the sum of the effects of the medicine and the alcohol) or even synergistic (more than the sum of the medicine and the alcohol). Concern has been expressed over the influence of marijuana on drivers. When combined with alcohol, marijuana can be a serious cause of impairment. Although other recreational drugs may play a role in traffic accidents, that traditional American favorite, alcohol, is still the major drug in the driver's seat.

It is obvious that alcohol has a profound impact on driving skill since it affects the ability of the brain to process information quickly and accurately. As a mind-altering drug, alcohol resembles sleeping pills and tranquilizers in that it acts as a depressant of the central nervous system.

Understanding BAC

Although the level of alcohol in a person can be tested in any body fluid that contains water—urine, saliva, blood, sweat and tears—blood has become the preferred medium. While drawing blood is a difficult procedure, nature makes testing blood alcohol levels easy. The thin membranes of the lungs are a border area where some of the alcohol in the blood stream passes through into the breath. There is a direct correlation between alcohol on the breath and alcohol in the blood that makes testing the breath an indicator of the blood level.

A blood alcohol concentration (BAC) is expressed as a percentage of alcohol to blood. One part of alcohol in 1,000 parts of blood would be a BAC of .10 percent, the point at which most states presume a driver to be "under the influence." A few states, however, have set their level lower, at .08 percent. Some others have a two-level system; the lower level constitutes a traffic offense, and higher level warrants a criminal charge.

In most states, a per se law means that you violate the law if you drive with a BAC level of .10 percent. From .05 to .09 you may still be found guilty of D[W]I on the basis of additional evidence. In these states, a BAC of below .05 means you are legally presumed not to be under the influence.

A hardened drinker may have a BAC of .10 and still not stagger, not slur his words. Does that mean he'll have no trouble driving?

Not according to the road test evidence. People who have built up a tolerance for alcohol can, after drinking, successfully perform the coordination test, pick up coins, whatever, and still be heavily impaired in terms of judgment, in terms of being able to react to a surprise on the road.

In talking about tolerance, however, we're talking about BAC's only at .03 or so. At .08 there seems to be a breaking point. Below that point there may be individuals who are not impaired, but above it, **everyone** is impaired. It is fair to say that at .10 percent BAC, anyone is impaired to the extent that he is a threat to society if he is behind the wheel of a car.

Source: *MADD Student Library* (A Publication of Mothers Against Drunk Driving, 1988), pp. 3–4.

Emotions, controlled by the brain's **limbic system**, are also distorted at this point, with results that include irrational sorrow or anger and excessive volubility.

A BAC of 0.4 percent causes coma, and a level of 0.5 percent depresses the **medulla oblongata**, the part of the brain stem that controls breathing, enough to cause death by respiratory failure in 2 or 3 hours. Even lower blood alcohol levels, those of approximately 0.4 percent, can be fatal if they are reached quite quickly, which is what happens when large quantities of alcohol are consumed in a very short period of time.

Limbic system: A set of structures in the brain that influences motivation and emotional behavior.

Medulla oblongata: A structure within the brain stem that helps regulate basic bodily functions such as breathing and heart rate.

ALCOHOL AND THE LIVER

Regardless of how much alcohol a person consumes, the body swings into action almost immediately to eliminate it. Minimal amounts of alcohol are excreted in the urine, perspiration, and

FIGURE 2.5
The Brain

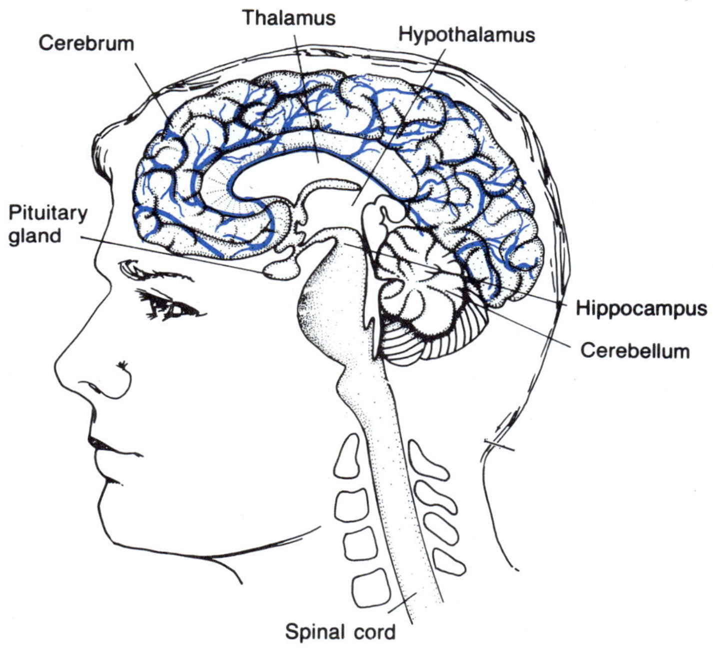

Source: T. Pettijohn, *Psychology: A Concise Introduction* 2d Edition (Guilford, CT: The Dushkin Publishing Group, 1989), p. 33.

Alcohol reaches the brain through the arterial network that transports the blood. All areas of the brain are affected by alcohol, including the cerebellum, which controls motor coordination, the hippocampus, which is responsible for memory and information retrieval, and the cerebral cortex, where cognitive processes take place.

breath, but for the most part the job of metabolizing, or breaking down, alcohol into less harmful substances falls to the **liver**, a remarkable organ located behind the ribs on the right side of the body. Its many functions include the formation of proteins, fats, and blood-clotting factors; detoxification of alcohol, drugs, and poisons, as well as toxic byproducts of metabolism, such as ammonia; the filtering and disposal of particles and organisms such as bacteria; storage of **glycogen**, which is a major source of

(continued on p. 37)

Liver: A soft, reddish-brown organ that is the largest gland in the body; its many important functions include the destruction of red blood cells, the regulation of carbohydrate metabolism, and the detoxification of drugs and other substances, including alcohol.

Glycogen: A form of complex carbohydrate stored in the body. It is found primarily in liver and muscle tissue.

Did You Know That . . .

Cirrhosis of the liver occurs about 8 times as often among heavy drinkers as among those who abstain from alcohol.

FIGURE 2.6
Alcohol's Path Through the Body

1. Mouth. Alcohol is drunk.

2. Stomach. Alcohol goes to stomach. Some goes through wall and into bloodstream, but most goes down into the small intestine.

3. Small Intestine. Most alcohol then goes through the walls of the intestine into the bloodstream.

4. Bloodstream. The bloodstream carries the alcohol to all parts of the body, such as brain, heart and liver.

5. Liver. The liver changes alcohol to water, carbon dioxide and energy at the rate of about one-half ounce per hour.

6. Brain. Alcohol goes to the brain almost as soon as it is drunk and keeps passing through the brain until the liver has had time to change all the alcohol into carbon dioxide, water and energy.

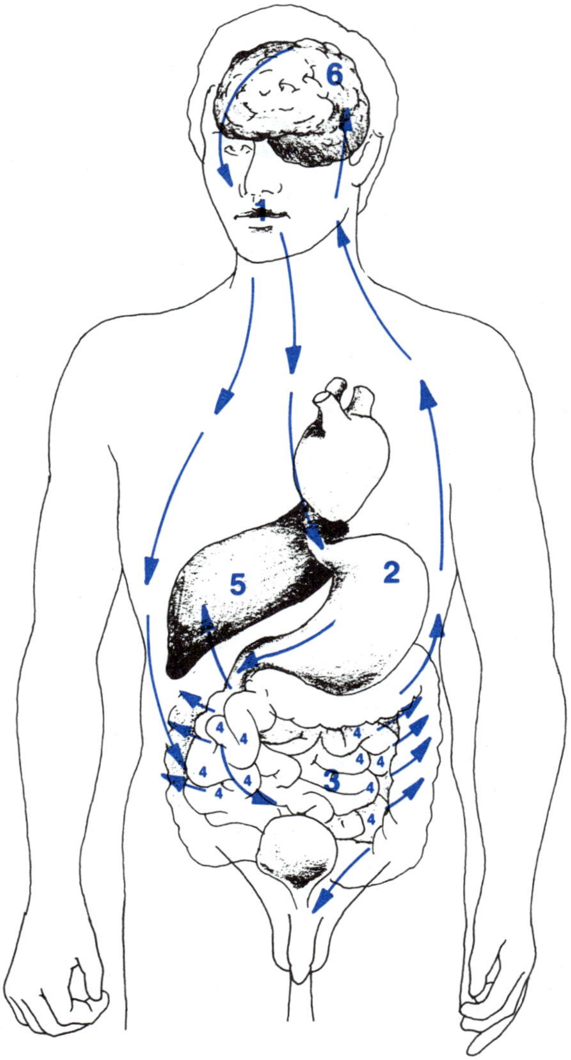

Source: *Alcohol's Effects,* MADD Student Library, 1988, pp. 3–4.

This diagram shows the path that alcohol takes once it enters the body.

energy, and of vitamins; and formation of the **bile** and bile acids used for digestion and absorption of nutrients.[10]

As soon as alcohol reaches the liver, this organ reacts to the alcohol molecules as foreign substances toxic (or poisonous) to the body's cells and attacks them with an enzyme called alcohol dehydrogenase (ADH). ADH removes two hydrogen atoms from the alcohol molecule to create a new substance called **acetaldehyde**. Since acetaldehyde is itself a highly toxic substance that can–when present in large quantities–produce rapid heartbeat, nausea, headache, disorientation, and dizziness, the liver continues the process that will in turn eliminate this **metabolite** from the body. To change acetaldehyde into **acetate**, the liver deploys the enzyme aldehyde dehydrogenase. Acetate is eventually converted into water and subsequently eliminated from the body.

The liver is able to process moderate amounts of alcohol quite efficiently, quickly converting it to acetate at the rate of about one-half ounce per hour. When large amounts of alcohol are present, however, the liver must work overtime to eliminate the alcohol and thus neglects its other vital functions, which include the elimination of other toxins from the body and meeting the nutritional needs of the body's cells.

In addition to the effect alcohol has on the liver and blood, it causes the cells to effect a physical adaptation. Heavy doses of alcohol slow down the activity level of cells; when this happens, cells gradually speed up their activity levels to compensate for the depressant effects of alcohol. This cellular adaptation is crucial to the continuation of all vital bodily processes in the presence of alcohol. Superficially, cells that have adapted to the presence of alcohol seem to be functioning normally; that is, their activity levels, when scientifically measured, are not very different from those of similar cells that have not been exposed to alcohol. However, cells that are compensating for the disruptions of alcohol are not functioning normally at all because they must work harder to maintain their usual activity levels. As alcohol is metabolized, the drug's effects gradually wear off. However, cellular activity does not slow down at the same rate. As alcohol is eliminated from the cells, therefore, their activity level undergoes a kind of rebound effect, in which they are operating at an abnormally high energy level. When millions of cells rebound simultaneously, the effect is quite dramatic. Moderate drinkers experience feelings of restlessness and anxiety. In alcohol abusers, this rebound effect is severe and includes severe shaking or tremors. [11]

Bile: A yellow or greenish liquid secreted by the liver, stored in the gallbladder, and released into the small intestine. It plays a major role in the metabolism of fats and the activation of other digestive enzymes.

Acetaldehyde: A colorless water-soluble liquid produced by the partial breakdown (oxidation) of ethanol, the active ingredient in alcoholic beverages; volatile and flammable (if exposed to air), it is also toxic.

Metabolite: Any chemical by-product of the metabolic process.

Acetate: A by-product (metabolite) of the body's breakdown of alcohol. It is chemically related to acetic acid.

As millions of "social drinkers" can attest, the body's ability to adapt to moderate amounts of alcohol is remarkable. The liver busily processes and eliminates this powerful drug with predict-

(continued on p. 40)

Did You Know That . . .

The life expectancy of alcohol drinkers is 10 to 12 years shorter than that of the general public.

Malignant melanoma: A highly malignant skin cancer originating in the pigment-secreting cells in the skin.

Congestive heart failure: A chronic disease of the heart characterized by greatly reduced pumping efficiency, accompanied by enlargement of the heart muscle and the buildup of fluid throughout the body.

Lipoproteins: A class of proteins found in the blood that consist of a simple protein combined with a lipid (fatty substances that are otherwise insoluble in water). They are transported throughout the body by the blood, and are one of the body's important sources of food energy.

Morphine: An opium derivative, sometimes used as a pain reliever, that produces a sense of euphoria in the user; prolonged use can lead to both physical and psychological dependence.

Endorphin: Any one of a related group of substances with a chemical structure similar to morphine. Endorphins are produced by the body (particularly by the nervous system) and relieve pain.

Altering Body and Mind

Some of the most serious diseases associated with chronic alcohol abuse include cancer of the liver, larynx, esophagus, stomach, colon and breast, as well as **malignant melanoma.** Alcoholism also leads to high blood pressure, stroke and heart attack; damage to the brain, pancreas and kidney (diabetes, renal failure); stomach and duodenal ulcers, colitis and irritable colon; birth defects and fetal alcohol syndrome; impotence and infertility; premature aging, and a host of other disorders such as muscle cramps, diminished immunity to disease, sleep disturbances, and edema. In fact, alcohol-related diseases account for 30 percent to 50 percent of all hospital admissions.

One recent study showed that a single high dose of alcohol in young nonalcoholic men depressed their heart's pumping ability much more than was previously thought. Still other studies have shown that, in an already damaged heart, alcohol can reduce the cardiac output enough to throw the person into **congestive heart failure.** Although some studies indicate that consuming one and a half ounces of liquor per day raises the count of blood **lipoproteins** that protect against heart attack, other experiments, especially with women, show conflicting results.

Heart specialists are thus divided in their opinions and generally cautious. "This is a swinging pendulum and you have to be very, very careful who[m] you are encouraging to drink," advises Dr. Isadore Rosenfeld, a well-known cardiologist at New York Hospital. "Anyone who tends to drink too much, or who has hypertension, or cardiac arrythmia—absolutely no drinking. Alcohol and cigarettes are the worst possible combination, greatly increasing the risk of heart disease and cancer."

This psychobiological path through the disease of alcoholism is full of subtle twists and turns. Some alcoholics, particularly those who drink small amounts throughout the day to maintain a constant glow, say they never feel "normal" until they have a drink.

One exciting, but controversial, area of neurochemical research has provided scientific clues to this mystery by linking alcohol with the opiate system in the central nervous system. Some animal experiments have suggested that alcohol is metabolized into opiate-like compounds, tetrahydroisoquinolines (TIQ's), which act on the same nerve receptors as do **morphine** and **endorphins,** the body's naturally produced opiates. Dr. Kenneth Blum of the University of Texas Health Science Center thinks that chronic heavy consumption of alcohol tricks the body into shutting down the natural production of endorphins, because its TIQ metabolites mimic the action of opiates. This robs the alcoholic, as soon as the high of alcohol wears off, of any normal feeling of well-being. On the basis of animal experiments, Dr. Blum believes that endorphin levels do not return to normal, even after long periods of abstinence, and that this might shed light on why sober alcoholics often have at least one relapse.

Dr. Blum goes several steps further. His experimental mice, bred through several generations to love alcohol though not yet exposed to it, also show low endorphin levels, and he believes some alcoholics are born with such a deficiency. Environmental stress has also been shown to lower the endorphin levels in rats and encourage them to drink. This might explain why some alcoholics with no family history of the disease develop it anyway, though usually later in life than those with alcoholic relatives.

Dr. Blum's work has been replicated in humans in Italy and Sweden, and, in this competitive, exploding field, his research and that of others working in the area of TIQ's have been the subject of acrimonious debate. "It is a very enticing theory, but it is just a beginning," says Dr. Tabakoff of the N.I.A.A.A. The theory that Dr. Tabakoff believes holds greater promise involves the reinforcing qualities of alcohol in the reward system of the brain. Some alcoholics, particularly episodic drinkers who down great amounts in one sitting, talk of a rush of intense euphoria, of sudden cosmic understanding, of sensations of power, brilliance and absolution. Experiments conducted on animals indicate that some alcoholics may have a metabolic anomaly which causes alcohol to stimulate pleasure more than in normal people, thereby creating a dependency.

Another research team has found that alcoholics are neurophysiologically vulnerable to intense sensory inputs, and may use alcohol to protect themselves from this supersensitivity. This would fit in with testimony by alcoholics that any dramatic experience, whether positive or negative, leads them to reach for a drink.

Whatever the **etiology** of the disease, it is clear that alcoholics develop increasing tolerance; indeed, the ability to drink larger and larger amounts is often a warning sign.

Once tolerance is developed, the slow change in the way the brain processes information begins. Alcoholics describe feelings of futility and meaninglessness and exhibit such signs of reality distortion as **paranoia,** aggressiveness, **narcissism,** extreme lack of confidence and an inability to accept criticism, or to see how their behavior is affecting others. Scientists are just beginning to discover neurochemical disruptions which might provide scientific explanations for these states of mind. . . .

Source: Lucinda Franks, "A New Attack on Alcoholism," *New York Times,* 20 October 1985, pp. 62–64.

Etiology: The scientific cause of a disease; also the study of the causes of disease generally.

Paranoia: A form of schizophrenia characterized by delusions of grandeur and a suspicion of others, particularly a strong belief that one or more other individuals are out to "get" the sufferer.

Narcissism: A preoccupation with and love of one's self and one's own physical or mental attributes.

able efficiency. Although brain activity is immediately and strongly affected by even small amounts of alcohol, its functioning quickly returns to normal once the alcohol is removed. However, when alcohol abuse occurs and the body is given more of this toxin than it can accommodate, the destructive by-products or metabolites of alcohol build up in all the body's organs. Both physical and mental pathologies then ensue, some of which are reversible up to a point. However, if left untreated, these pathologies can be deadly. We will examine these pathologies in detail in chapter 4, which deals with the many harmful effects of alcohol abuse and alcoholism.

CHAPTER

3

The Staggering Toll

THERE ARE approximately 10 to 13 million alcoholics in the United States; in addition, experts estimate that there are more than 7 million alcohol abusers. [1] As a result of alcohol abuse, problem drinkers suffer impaired performance on the job, accidental injuries, and other medical disorders. Alcoholism is involved in 60 percent of reported cases of child abuse and in the majority of cases of spouse abuse. Alcohol is currently implicated in nearly half of all accidental deaths, suicides, and homicides in the United States, including 42 percent of all deaths from motor vehicle accidents. Alcohol-related **cirrhosis** of the liver is the ninth leading cause of death, with an annual toll of 27,000 lives. In 1984, more than 500,000 Americans were being treated for alcohol abuse and alcoholism. [2]

Some estimates place the annual cost of alcohol abuse to American society as high as $128.3 billion. [3] Alcoholics make up a disproportionate percentage of the population in the nation's prisons, mental institutions, and hospitals. In terms of lost production, alcohol costs industry more than $60 billion a year; health and medical costs run more than $16.5 billion; motor vehicle losses more than $5 billion; violent crime $3 billion; and fire at least $340 million. If the hidden costs of undiagnosed and unrecognized alcoholism were factored in, the totals would be even higher. [4]

Cirrhosis: A degenerative disease of the liver characterized by the accumulation of large fatty deposits and scar tissue that impairs functioning; the major causes of cirrhosis are chronic liver inflammation, hepatitis B, and chronic alcoholism.

WHO DRINKS?

Who are these alcoholics? Old movies often depict the typical problem drinker as a skid-row male bum sidling from bar to bar.

FIGURE 3.1
Estimated Percentage of Alcohol Related Deaths by Cause

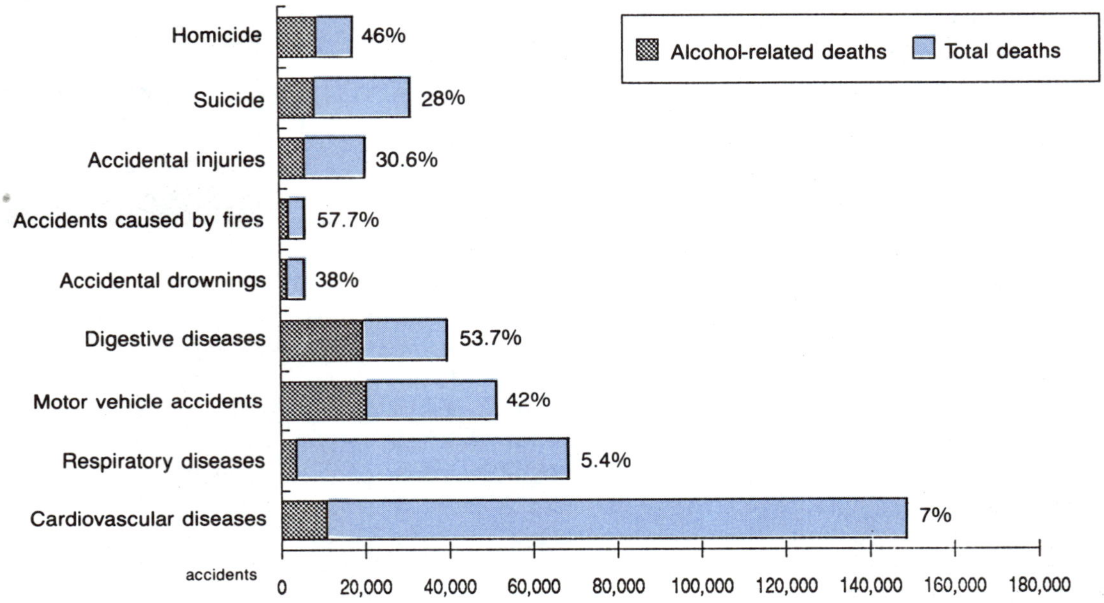

Source: Centers for Disease Control, *Morbidity and Mortality Weekly Report* 39, No. 11 (23 March 1990), p. 174.

The true cost of alcohol abuse is hard to determine, but is often far greater than is immediately apparent. As the above graph suggests, many deaths attributed to other causes are in fact alcohol-related.

In truth, victims of alcoholism cover a much wider spectrum. To be sure, a large percentage of the nation's alcoholics are adult men, but the disease affects both men and women from all races and economic classes.

About one-third of the country's 10 to 13 million alcoholics are women. [5] This is a fairly recent phenomenon. Many bars in the early part of the century did not allow women to drink, and only since the mid-1970s have scientists studied alcohol problems among women. Studies show that although it is impossible to produce a single description for female alcoholics, there do tend to be some patterns. For example, according to research, women are more likely to drink heavily if they are unmarried, unemployed, or working part-time. [6] But women in full-time positions are also susceptible.

FIGURE 3.2
Women and Alcohol

The number of women with alcohol-related problems is steadily rising. More than 60 percent of American women now drink alcoholic beverages. Of those, it is estimated that 12 to 16 percent are heavy drinkers.

Stress is known to be tied to alcohol **addiction**. Men who are in high-power jobs are quite susceptible to stress and its consequences—high blood pressure, heart problems, and the like. Women who have the same jobs are subject to the same stresses and often face others as well. The notion that women should also be family caretakers, even if employed outside of the home, is an unrealistic expectation, and one that can overburden a woman in

(continued on p. 45)

Stress: Any outside influence or event that produces a demand on the individual to adjust; stress may be either positive or negative.

Addiction: A chronic, compulsive, or uncontrollable craving for and dependence on a particular substance or activity.

Did You Know That . . .

The percentage of mothers who drink while pregnant dropped from 32 percent in 1985 to 20 percent in 1988.

In ancient Rome, the use of alcohol by women was forbidden. By Roman law, women caught drinking were sentenced to death—by methods such as stoning or starvation.

Times have changed. However, alcohol use continues to pose a special health threat to women.

Alcohol Abuse Among Women

The number of women with alcohol abuse problems—including teenagers and women in their 20s—has dramatically risen over the past 40 years. More than 60 percent of American women now drink alcoholic beverages, the highest percentage ever. Of those, it is estimated that 12 to 16 percent are heavy drinkers (three to five drinks a day). And new evidence suggests that heavy drinking is on the rise among young, employed women.

Women afflicted with alcoholism tend to be less visible than men. Many drink at home and alone. Therefore, alcohol abuse among women has been called a "hidden" or "invisible" problem.

Although women drink less and have lower rates of alcohol problems than men, their alcohol-related health hazards may be greater. Alcohol abuse among women is an important health issue that only recently has begun to receive attention. As a society, we must learn to recognize women who may be at risk of developing problems when they drink, and become aware of danger signals when they occur.

What Causes Alcoholism?

Alcohol addiction researchers say heredity and family background may predispose women (and men) to alcohol abuse.

Who, exactly, is an alcoholic? There is no simple answer to this question because symptoms are not always clear-cut. Extreme cases are obvious, but often symptoms are less dramatic.

Women alcoholics, like their male counterparts, often suffer from feelings of inadequacy, low self-esteem and extreme guilt. Also, they may be victims of incest, rape, child or spouse abuse or be daughters of alcoholic parents. Women (and men) from families in which alcohol led to problems are much more likely to develop a drinking problem.

Marital discord, **depression, anxiety** and child-rearing difficulties all provide a milieu in which alcoholism can thrive. Factors unique to women, such as severe premenstrual changes in mood, **postpartum depression** and **menopause,** have been mentioned as possible causes for alcohol abuse in women, but clear documentation is lacking. Some specialists propose that sex role conflicts and tensions also may contribute to the drinking problems of women.

Depression: A mental state characterized by extreme sadness or dejection, both far out of proportion to the reality of the situation over which the sufferer is depressed.

Anxiety: An emotional state characterized by general uneasiness, apprehension, or fear.

Postpartum depression: A depressed state experienced by some mothers shortly after the birth of a child.

Menopause: The period during which a woman's menstrual cycle ceases for normal reasons; the "change of life."

Concealment Is a Problem

Historically, female alcoholics have faced a harsher stigma than male alcoholics. For fear of both social disapproval and personal abandonment, women often go to great lengths to hide their drinking problems. They become "closet drinkers," less apt to be confronted about their drinking problems. Consequently, the degree of problem drinking among women has been underestimated by science and society.

Also, family and friends may try to conceal or deny a woman's alcohol abuse because they are embarrassed by or protective of her situation. Many women alcoholics go untreated. Either their condition is undetected or the women are "protected" by well-meaning family and friends who deny or suppress the problem. Efforts at dealing with alcohol abuse have been mainly directed at the workplace—excluding a significant number of women. . . .

Source: *Mayo Clinic Health Letter*, July 1988, pp. 5–6.

Did You Know That . . .

About 66 percent of all American adults drink alcoholic beverages, and about 6.5 percent of those adults account for at least half of the total alcohol consumption in the United States.

such a position. As a reaction to the additional strain, such a woman may start depending upon mild, "acceptable" substances, such as minor tranquilizers or alcohol to ease the burden. If she is not careful, this dependence can lead to addiction.

Alcohol consumption is also a problem for teenagers. In one 1988 study, 92 percent of all adolescents had at least tried alcohol. [7] A 1985 survey showed that 30 percent of teenagers had gotten drunk at least once in the past month. [8] It is quite difficult to pinpoint the exact reasons any given teenager begins to drink. Genetic and environmental factors may play a role. There are, however, several mitigating factors worth discussing. Adolescence is a time of mixed feelings and intense change. It is also a time of rebellion. Teenagers often seek extracurricular activities that may help ease the intense emotions that so often overcome them. Some teens exercise, play music, or take art classes. Some young people, however, find that the best way to forget their troubles–and/or to rebel against authority figures–is to drink.

Because it is easily available–many teenagers can find alcohol in their family refrigerators or liquor cabinets–alcohol is the drug of choice at many teen parties. At such events, many adolescents are apt to drink if their friends do. Peer pressure is an ever-present phenomenon during adolescence, and a teenager may find it easier to accept the challenge and have a drink or 2 than to say no and face the consequences. Doing so may seem like the less difficult choice, but it can have dire consequences. Drunk driving, discussed later on in this chapter, kills thousands of teenagers every year. In addition, early alcohol use can lead to more serious consequences, either with alcohol or other drugs.

Did You Know That . . .

When a group of high school-age boys were asked to name their favorite television commercials, the most popular choices were beer ads.

Sobering Facts

Although many adults chuckle over their first experiments with alcohol, youthful drinking is no joke. Consider:

- The average age for beginning to drink is 12.
- Alcohol is the most commonly used drug among adolescents.
- By senior year in high school, one out of every 20 students drinks daily.
- Nearly half of all teens who commit suicide are intoxicated at the time.
- In 1986, more than 3,500 teens died in alcohol-related car crashes.
- Nearly one out of every three teens reports riding with an adolescent driver who was drunk.
- Although 93 percent of children in grades 4–6 say that cocaine is a drug, only 21 percent think wine coolers are drugs.

Source: *Better Homes and Gardens,* May 1988, p. 72.

Teenage alcoholism is a frightening, contemporary problem; unlike drug use, it has not yet begun to decline. Educators are hopeful, however, that with increased awareness and additional programs, teenagers will find healthier outlets and activities for their formidable energy.

Alcoholism among the elderly is yet another problem in modern society. According to various studies, 10 to 15 percent of those over 60 abuse alcohol. [9] In such cases, specific events will often trigger an increased reliance on alcohol. Such events include retirement, loss of a spouse, or entry into a nursing home. The onset of a debilitating illness, marital problems, or increasing loneliness can also play a role in elderly alcoholism.

WORKING UNDER THE INFLUENCE OF ALCOHOL

Even conservative estimates of the impact of alcoholism and other drug abuse on the workplace are staggering. The National Institute on Drug Abuse (NIDA) and the National Institute on Alcohol Abuse and Alcoholism estimate that at least 10 percent of the work force is afflicted by alcoholism or drug addiction.

Another 10 to 15 percent is affected by the substance abuse of a member of their immediate family. [10] Active alcoholics are a major drain on any company's resources, hurting productivity, undermining employee morale, and posing a dire threat to their own safety and to that of their fellow workers. Even when a worker is not actually drunk on the job, he or she may be suffering from the aftereffects of a drinking binge and, consequently, be seriously impaired.

Alcoholism on the job is by no means confined to blue-color or semiskilled workers. Since the 1970s, problems of alcoholism among professionals have received considerable attention. For example, in *Confessions of a Medical Heretic,* published in 1979, Dr. Robert S. Mendelsohn reported that "conservative counts peg the number of alcoholic doctors in the United States at more than

(continued on p. 49)

Workers' Substance Abuse Is Increasing, Survey Says

Executives and Federal officials say the use of cocaine and crack is growing rapidly among workers, significantly compounding the effects of drug and alcohol abuse, which cost business more than $100 billion a year.

[According to a 1988 survey], 42 percent of the employers who responded said that 6 to 10 percent of their employees have an alcohol or drug problem and 12 percent of the employers said that 11 to 15 percent of their employees have such problems.

Absenteeism, medical expenses and lost productivity are costing employers an average of 3 percent of their total payroll. In comparison, the typical company's payments for an employee's Social Security coverage is 6.1 percent of its payroll.

"Things are getting worse," said Dr. Robert G. Wiencek, general director of occupational safety and health at the General Motors Corporation, citing the increase in cocaine addiction.

"The individual who is using cocaine is unsafe," Dr. Wiencek said. "He uses very poor judgment." Because of distorted thinking, "the quality of his work is frequently diminished."

Substance abuse among G.M.'s 472,000 workers and their dependents cost the automotive company $600 million [in 1987].

The growing concern is evident in recent surveys, other studies and interviews with executives and Government officials.

The survey . . . found that the situation ha[d] . . . worsened in the [preceding] five years. It was conducted by a consulting firm that compiled the responses of 224 corporate chiefs, 18 state governors and 23 mayors of large cities. Seventy-nine percent of the officials who responded identified drugs and alcohol as significant or very significant problems in their organizations, but only 54 percent of the employers said this had been the case five years ago.

The Federal Government, meanwhile, estimates that alcohol and drug abuse costs the economy $177 billion a year, including $99 billion attributed to lost productivity. Two-thirds of the cost is attributed to alcohol. In the construction industry alone, the cost amounts to $10 billion, University of Michigan researchers said [November 1988] in a separate study.

One expert calculates that the cost may be even higher. "Lost productivity attributable to drugs and alcohol amounts to $1,000 per worker per year in the United States, or $120 billion for 120 million workers," said Dr. Robert L. DuPont, a consultant and former director of the National Institute on Drug Abuse.

Although drug and alcohol use among high school students has stopped increasing—and in the case of heavy use of marijuana, has apparently declined—millions of adults who started drinking or taking drugs in the 1960's and 1970's have joined the work force.

They are still struggling to stay in control of their lives while holding jobs, Dr. DuPont said.

Small Companies Also Hurt

While General Motors and its $600 million tab [in 1987] may seem outsize, other companies have also been hit with heavy charges. At least seven companies said they calculated the cost of alcohol and drug abuse at more than $50 million each, according to the survey of 224 companies conducted by the Mercer Meidinger Hansen division of the Marsh & McLennan Companies, the insurance and consulting firm.

Fifty-four percent of the executives said their companies tested the urine of job applicants for signs of drugs. Thirty-one percent said they also tested incumbent employees, usually after behavior viewed as impaired or when safety was involved.

Only a few companies test employees at random. Fifty-seven percent of the chief executives said they do not favor random testing.

Mercer Meidinger sent questionnaires to the heads of the Fortune 1,000 companies, the 50 governors and the mayors of the 64 largest cities. Responses were received from about one quarter of those solicited. The replies came from a broad range of industries, including automobiles, banking, chemicals, communications, computers, energy, food products, insurance, petroleum, retailing and transportation.

Similar concerns were expressed by senior executives in interviews.

Definite Increase

"There is definitely an increase in substance abuse taking place," said Stephen L. Brown, president of the John Hancock Mutual Life Insurance Company. The increased awareness may be partly "a reflection of people everywhere becoming more open about the problems," he said.

On Wall Street, at least 15 of the largest firms have started drug testing and counseling programs in the last few years, after "a number of thefts and frauds in the industry were connected to drugs," said Edward Weihenmayer, a former chairman of the Wall Street Personnel Managers Association.

"Double-digit numbers of people were terminated at premier firms, usually lower-level people such as messengers," said Mr. Weihenmayer, who recently moved to Salomon Brothers as managing director in charge of human resources. "I was aware of six- and seven-figure losses connected to drug use."

Spread of Crack-Cocaine

"Crack-cocaine . . . spread across the country in the last six months [of 1988] from the major drug-using cities—New York, Los Angeles and Miami—to places far from the entry ports like Des Moines and Wheeling, W. Va.," said J. Michael Walsh, director of the Office of Workplace Initiatives at the National Institute on Drug Abuse, a Federal agency. Crack is a smokable form of cocaine.

"The availability of crack-cocaine has made addicts out of people at a much more rapid rate," he said. It may take up to "10 to 12 years for an alcoholic to become totally dysfunctional," or unable to work, he said. "But we are seeing people who have been using crack-cocaine for short periods of only six to eight weeks who are unable to get up and go to work."

Marijuana and cocaine were the most frequently abused drugs other than alcohol reported in another recent survey, of 1,238 employers, by the Human Interaction Research Institute, a nonprofit group headed by Dr. Backer. "Multiple drug abuse—cocaine and alcohol" was even more frequent than cocaine used alone, he said.

"The misuse of alcohol is still the greatest drug

problem facing employers," said Bryan Lawton, a vice president at the Wells Fargo Bank in San Francisco. He said alcohol is twice as costly for employers as other drugs and "twice as prevalent, because it is socially acceptable."

Testing for Drugs

Many companies test for drugs when safety is involved. For example, Dr. Bruce W. Karrh, vice president of safety and health affairs at Du Pont, said workers on "safety-sensitive jobs" will be tested at random at new plants in Orange, Tex., and Belle, W. Va.

The Federal Department of Transportation has ordered drug testing of airline pilots, train and bus drivers and other transportation industry employees, where the public may be at risk.

But random testing is rare, both because of concerns about privacy and the expense involved. "If you consider the size of G.M. and you were to do random drug screening of 100 employees before you found 10 positive—at $25 a test, that's a very small yield for a very high price," Dr. Wiencek said. "There has to be a better way."

A few companies are aggressive about testing. For example, the Georgia Power Company, which has long had employee counseling programs and testing for safety reasons, recently started random testing.

"Employees found to be involved with drugs were responsible for a significant number of accidents," said Howard Winkler, labor relations coordinator at Georgia Power, a subsidiary of the Southern Company.

—*Milt Freudenheim*

Source: Milt Freudenheim, *New York Times,* 12 December 1988, sec. 4, pp. 1, 5.

30,000." [11] Alcoholism and substance abuse are also widespread among nurses and pharmacists; in fact, Dr. Madeline Naegle, chairperson of the American Nursing Association's Committee on Impaired Nursing Practice, stated in 1986 that between 5 and 6 percent, or 100,000, of 1.9 million registered nurses in the United States abuse alcohol and/or other drugs. [12]

The problem of alcohol abuse among workers with responsibilities for public safety is especially grave. These include airplane pilots, air-traffic controllers, bus drivers, train engineers, workers in nuclear power plants, and so forth. The Federal Aviation Agency, the Airline Medical Department, and the Airline Pilots Association recognized alcoholism as a problem among pilots in 1973. At that time, these 3 groups set up an alcohol rehabilitation program for pilots and persuaded professionals to volunteer for treatment if necessary. Eight years later, the program was able to report that at least 300 pilots had sought help to cope with their illness.

In 1986 the Federal Aviation Agency became concerned enough about alcohol abuse among pilots and crews to consider random testing for alcohol and other substance abuse. "Drug and alcohol abuse is a major problem in society," stated an FAA report. "The alcohol abuse among personnel engaged in aviation activities is not any lesser or greater than that of the general public." [13] Needless to say, however, a pilot who works under the influence of alcohol or any other drug puts a far greater number of people at risk than does a business executive or shoe salesman. "Where the safe transportation of the public is concerned," stated then-Secretary of Transportation Elizabeth Dole, "there can be no tolerance for drug or alcohol abuse." [14]

Perhaps the most tragic and notorious example of the consequences that alcohol abuse can have on society at large occurred on March 23, 1989. On that day, the *Exxon Valdez,* a 210,000-ton, 987-foot oil tanker carrying 1.3 million barrels of crude oil, ran aground in Alaska's Prince William Sound. The spill took place in one of the most sensitive marine life areas in the world, creating an environmental catastrophe of unprecedented dimensions. Five hundred square miles of the Sound were despoiled, disrupting for generations the economic and recreational life of the region.

The captain of the *Exxon Valdez* was Joseph Hazelwood, who had left the navigation of treacherous waters to an inexperienced third mate. Hazelwood had a history of alcoholism, and blood tests taken 9 hours after the accident indicated that Hazelwood had been intoxicated at that time. Although Hazelwood was subsequently acquitted of felony charges brought against him, there is no dispute that he failed to meet his responsibilities when he abandoned the bridge of the ship at a critical point in its voyage and that there was sufficient evidence to charge him with operating a motor craft under the influence of alcohol and with reckless endangerment.

DRINKING AND DRIVING

Over the past 2 decades, the life expectancy of every age group in this country has risen, with the exception of adolescents. Motor vehicle accidents are largely to blame, accounting for 45 percent of teenage deaths. Other accidents, such as drownings and falls, account for only 13 percent. Among teenagers who die in car accidents, nearly 60 percent are under the influence of alcohol at the time of the accident. In 1984, 9,000 people between the ages of 15 and 24 died in car crashes in which drinking was involved. Another 22,000 were injured, many disabled and maimed for life. [15]

It goes without saying that drunk driving victimizes not only teenagers but all Americans. Despite the fact that alcohol is the number-one killer on the road, many Americans persist in the

FIGURE 3.3
Blood Alcohol Concentrations and Fatally Injured Drivers

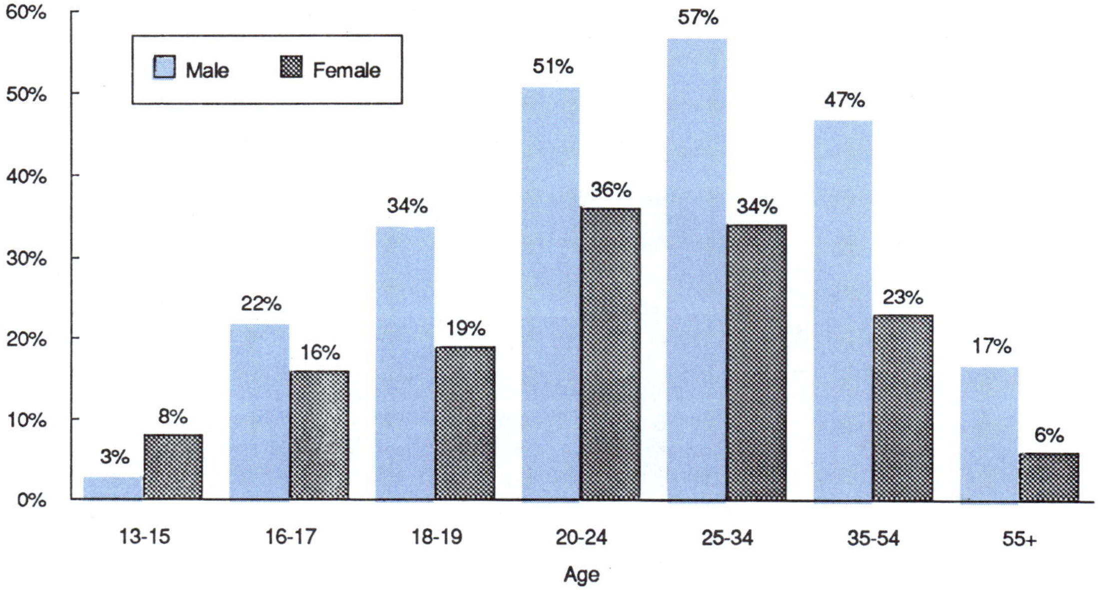

Source: Insurance Institute for Highway Safety, *IIHS Facts,* Arlington, VA, 1989.

Automobile accidents kill over 50,000 Americans annually, and a significant proportion of these deaths are alcohol-related. As this chart indicates, the percentage of fatally injured drivers with blood alcohol concentrations in excess of 0.10 is greatest among the 20–24, 25–34, and 35–54 age groups.

conviction that they can drive safely while under the influence. A 1985 Gallup poll showed that as many as one-third of the nation's drinkers have gotten behind the wheel of a car after they had been drinking. [16] The U.S. Department of Transportation estimates that on any given weekend, 10 percent of the drivers on the road are legally intoxicated.

However, despite the fact that adults and adolescents alike make the potentially fatal mistake of driving while impaired by alcohol, most of drunk driving's fatal victims are young people. Young people between the ages of 15 and 24 represent only 20 percent of the licensed drivers in this country, but they are involved in 42 percent of all fatal alcohol-related crashes. While driving under the influence of alcohol, teenage drinkers are up to

Did You Know That . . .

When 1,500 tavern and nightclub goers were surveyed, 75 percent said they felt confident they would be able to drive safely while intoxicated.

3 times more likely to be involved in a fatal car accident than are older drivers. This tragic fact is easily explained by the fact that young people are usually both inexperienced drinkers and inexperienced drivers, are more radically affected by the effects of

Alcohol Tied to the Deaths of 105,095 in U.S. in '87

ATLANTA, March 26 (AP)—The national Centers for Disease Control has reported that 105,095 Americans died from injuries or diseases linked to alcoholic beverages in 1987. . . .

The leading alcohol-related cause of death was injuries, chiefly in auto wrecks involving a drunken driver.

Unintentional injuries related to alcohol killed 30,205 Americans in 1987, 29 percent of alcohol-related deaths. Second were digestive diseases, including alcoholic cirrhosis of the liver. Those diseases killed 19,556 people.

"This does not mean a problem for everyone who drinks," said Dr. James Shultz of the University of Miami School of Medicine, the chief researcher for the report, which was issued [in March 1990]. Millions of people drink, he said, "so a minority of those who drink have a fatal outcome."

ALMOST 300 DEATHS A DAY

But the alcohol-related deaths, nearly 300 a day, mean that "alcohol is a major problem," Dr. Shultz said. "Now, it's for policy-makers to assess that problem," and set policy, he said.

Studies of alcohol-related sickness and death are subject to much conjecture over what "alcohol-related" should mean—binge drunkenness, heavy drinking or even moderate, life-long drinking, Dr. Shultz said.

His study used estimates from previous research for various conditions: For example, mouth cancer deaths are believed alcohol-related 50 percent of the time, and respiratory tuberculosis deaths are alcohol-related 25 percent of the time.

Even then, researchers disagree over the question of how much drinking makes someone's death "alcohol-related," and not simply the natural death of someone who drank.

But Dr. Shultz said most deaths from alcohol fall into two patterns: sudden, violent deaths from a dangerous drunken episode, and long-term, debilitating, heavy drinking that brings on disease.

"If we had everyone who drinks drinking very occasionally, at levels not likely to produce injury-prone, dangerous behavior, you'd have very few alcohol-related deaths," he said.

Source: *New York Times,* 27 March 1990, sec. 3, p. C10.

FIGURE 3.4

Blood Alcohol Concentration and Body Weight

Approximate Blood Alcohol Percentage

Drinks	Body Weight in Pounds								
	100	120	140	160	180	200	220	240	
1	.04	.03	.03	.02	.02	.02	.02	.02	Possibly
2	.08	.06	.05	.05	.04	.04	.03	.03	Influenced
3	.11	.09	.08	.07	.06	.06	.05	.05	
4	.15	.12	.11	.09	.08	.08	.07	.06	
5	.19	.16	.13	.12	.11	.09	.09	.08	Under the
6	.22	.19	.16	.14	.13	.11	.10	.09	Influence
7	.26	.22	.19	.16	.15	.13	.12	.11	
8	.30	.25	.21	.19	.17	.15	.14	.13	
9	.34	.28	.24	.21	.19	.17	.15	.14	Intoxicated
10	.38	.31	.27	.23	.21	.19	.17	.16	

(Based on approximately 1 hour)

One drink equals:
1 oz. of 80 proof liquor
12 oz. of beer
4 oz. of wine (12% alcohol)

Caution: Many drinks have more than 1 oz. of alcohol.

Source: Connecticut Department of Transportation, Office of Highway Safety.

This chart shows the relationship between the number of drinks consumed by adults, their body weight, and blood alcohol concentration. Individuals may vary somewhat in their personal alcohol tolerance. Food in the stomach affects the rate of absorption. Medications, health, and psychological condition are also factors.

alcohol on reaction time and coordination, are frequently prone to reckless driving, and are often destabilized by the emotional storms of adolescence.

Although various anti-drunk driving crusades that began during the 1980s are beginning to bear fruit in a decrease in the rate of alcohol-related traffic accidents and fatalities, alcohol-impaired driving remains the leading cause of death among youths between the ages of 15 and 24. This age group also has a special vulnerability to alcohol-related traffic accidents in general. Moreover, there is a pattern indicating which teenagers are likely to be involved in these accidents. Young people between the ages of 16 and 24 who drive while under the influence of alcohol

FIGURE 3.5
Drunk Driving Kills

Nearly half of all traffic deaths are alcohol-related. Driving under the influence can result in poor judgment, slowed reaction time, loss of concentration, and visual problems. Nationwide, about 25,000 lives could be saved each year if people did not drink and drive.

are preponderantly male; they tend to be frequent binge drinkers, and they do a lot of their drinking while driving around in their cars for "recreation." [17] The high schoolers tend to be average students. Those out of high school are already experiencing serious social and personal problems caused by their heavy drinking and are either unemployed or working in low-skill jobs.

As experts look for causes and possible solutions to the carnage alcohol creates on the nation's highways, a profile of the typical drunk driver emerges. Contrary to popular opinion, most people of any age who drive while intoxicated are not social drinkers, but alcoholics. This is particularly true in the case of repeat offenders. Some studies indicate that out of every 1,000 convictions for drunk driving, 78 to 82 percent of the offenders are alcoholics, and only 18 to 22 percent are social drinkers. [18]

As society's awareness of the consequences of alcohol abuse for the nation as a whole has grown, so have the strategies, programs, and policies for coping with it. In chapters 5 and 6, we will discuss the multipronged attack that employers, lawmakers, citizens' groups, and professional alcoholism **therapists** and counselors are launching against one of the country's most serious health and safety issues.

Therapist: An individual who is trained in the treatment of one or more types of mental or physical disorder.

CHAPTER

4

The Individual Victim

AS WE SAW IN CHAPTER 1, alcoholism was not recognized as a disease until well into the twentieth century. Even today, many people still tend to view the person who chronically drinks to excess and suffers the consequent disruptions of his or her personal and social existence as somehow deficient in character and will. By the same token, experts in the field of alcoholism are sharply divided on the exact nature of this malady and hold conflicting opinions on whether it is primarily a physical or mental illness and how best to treat it.

Among those who hold that alcoholism is primarily a physical illness with emotional and psychological ramifications, a fundamental distinction is made between "problem" or heavy drinking and alcoholism. According to this distinction, problem drinkers are those who use alcohol inappropriately to manage chronic or acute stress, to compensate for feelings of inadequacy, as a function of narcissism, or as part of an over-all pattern of **obsessive-compulsive behavior**. Alcoholics, on the other hand, are victims of a genetically- or biologically-induced progressive physical disease. Whereas the problem drinker can learn to moderate his or her drinking as new methods of coping with emotional disturbances are acquired, the true alcoholic can never learn to drink moderately and may continue to drink in the face of overwhelming evidence that alcohol itself has become the primary cause of all his or her woes.

Obsessive-compulsive behavior: Behavior in which the individual seeks to control recurrent and persistent anxiety-evoking thoughts by repetitive actions.

(continued on p. 57)

Factors for Alcoholism

Why Do People Have Problems with Alcohol?

Some people drink and do not have problems. Other people drink and do have problems. What accounts for the difference? How can you know if you're likely to have a problem with alcohol—or, if you think you might have a problem, what makes *you* different from other people who drink but don't have a problem?

We know that the difference does not depend on who you are or where you live. Problems with alcohol occur in all racial groups, at all levels of society, and in all types of homes. But we also know that if you are a male and have a close male relative who is an alcoholic (a father or a brother), you have as much as a one out of two chance of becoming an alcoholic yourself. Despite that statistical probability, however, there is no scientific way of predicting in advance whether you are the one who will develop alcoholism or the other who will not.

Fortunately, the study of drug dependency and alcoholism has progressed to the point that we are beginning to understand various factors that do affect your drinking pattern and how you handle alcohol.

Factor #1: Your Genetic Inheritance

The first of these is your genes—the physical traits you inherit from your parents. It seems that some people, because of their genetic heritage, are predisposed to an inability to handle alcohol, much as some people inherit a tendency to develop diabetes or hypertension.

This is not a hard and fast rule, and it does not mean that the children of an alcoholic will *necessarily* develop the same problem. It simply means that some people may have, from birth, a decreased ability to process alcohol, and that this trait can be passed from one generation to the next.

Factor #2: Where and How You Grew Up

Another risk factor is the environment in which you learn to drink. If you have been exposed to drinking as an adult activity in which the drinkers are careful and moderate in their alcohol use, you are more likely to become the same kind of responsible drinker. If you grew up seeing alcohol used heavily, you are more likely to use alcohol that way yourself.

Factor #3: The Amount You Drink

Obviously, if you never drink or drink rarely, physical dependence cannot develop. If you drink a moderate amount—one to three drinks a day, just about every day—alcohol is probably already a habit with you. Whether or not it is a destructive habit depends on other factors, as we shall see.

But be aware that this is the point at which social drinkers can develop problems. Moderate drinkers are the ones who both enjoy drinking substantially and regularly, and who also believe that they can handle it. And indeed, they often can. But if other factors develop—including a carelessness about paying attention to how much and how often you drink—*the step across the line to alcohol dependency is a short one.*

People who drink heavily—three or four drinks a day or more—are often already dependent on alcohol. As noted, this is because **alcohol is an addictive substance; it causes reactions in the brain that the brain comes to depend on and to demand.** When an addictive substance is withdrawn, the body reacts in ways that make you feel you must have some, immediately. When the brain reaches the point that it depends on alcohol, you are no longer in control. Instead, you have a physical condition which controls you. Addiction happens when your body becomes so accustomed to a regular intake of alcohol that it must continue to have it, and any break in the flow causes real discomfort.

Factor #4: The Reason You Drink

The *reason* you drink is the factor which can tip the balance between social drinking and problem drinking. Many people start off using alcohol as a way of socializing or of celebrating. Some people find that because of stresses in their lives they feel better when they're on alcohol than when they're not. Alcohol then becomes a way of feeling good, a way of escaping the bad feelings caused by life's problems. When the drinker uses alcohol for escape in this way, he is adding psychological dependence—the emotional need for alcohol—to the physical one. Both the body and the mind depend on alcohol and even when it becomes clear that drink is causing more problems than it's solving, the need persists.

Factor #5: Your Knowledge of Alcohol and Yourself

The responsibility you bring to your drinking also has an effect on your potential for the misuse and abuse of alcohol. People who understand alcohol and its risks pay attention to how much, when, and why they drink. A social drinker might say, "I've been drinking a lot lately. I'm going to cut back," and then do it. People who have problems with alcohol tend to be unaware of how much they drink, how important it has become to them, or why. Inattention and carelessness allow habits to develop that the drinker never wanted.

Addiction and/or alcoholic drinking, then, develop as a result of several factors—the amount of drinking, the reasons for drinking, the attitudes developed in youth, even genetic heritage. Only one or two of these factors can be enough to cause problems. . . .

Source: *How to Assess Your Drinking* (Weymouth, MA: Life Skills Education, 1989), pp. 3–6.

Alcoholism was officially labeled a disease in 1956 by the American Medical Association and again in 1969 by the American College of Physicians. In 1960 E. B. Jellinek, a pioneer researcher and theorist on the subject of alcohol-related disorders, described several types of alcoholism, two of which he characterized as diseases: **gamma alcoholism** and **delta alcoholism**. The gamma alcoholic, who is unable to control the amount he or she drinks once the drinking has started, alternates between periods of uncontrollable drinking binges and complete abstinence. Delta alcoholics, on the other hand, are rarely able to abstain from drinking. They generally drink less than gamma alcoholics and on the surface seem to function better. However, delta alcoholics frequently drink throughout the day and are as vulnerable to the damage caused by heavy drinking as the periodic bingers are. [1]

In both types of alcoholism, the drinker develops a **tolerance** for alcohol, meaning that the body gradually becomes less and less sensitive to the effects of alcohol as usage continues and increases. Another characteristic of both gamma and delta alcoholism is **metabolic adaptation**, a process by which the body alters metabolic activity–the various ways in which the cells transform energy and matter into the materials necessary to sustain life–to adapt to the presence of high levels of alcohol in the blood and organs.

Gamma alcoholism: Alcoholism characterized by an inability to stop drinking once consumption of alcohol has started.

Delta alcoholism: Alcoholism characterized by an inability to abstain from drinking.

Tolerance: The gradual desensitization of the body to the effects of alcohol.

Metabolic adaptation: Any adjustment in the body's normal metabolic processes undertaken in response to a persistent or long-standing abnormal condition.

Did You Know That . . .

An estimated 20 to 40 percent of all U.S. hospital beds are occupied by persons suffering from complications of alcohol abuse and dependence.

FIGURE 4.1
Alcohol Tolerance

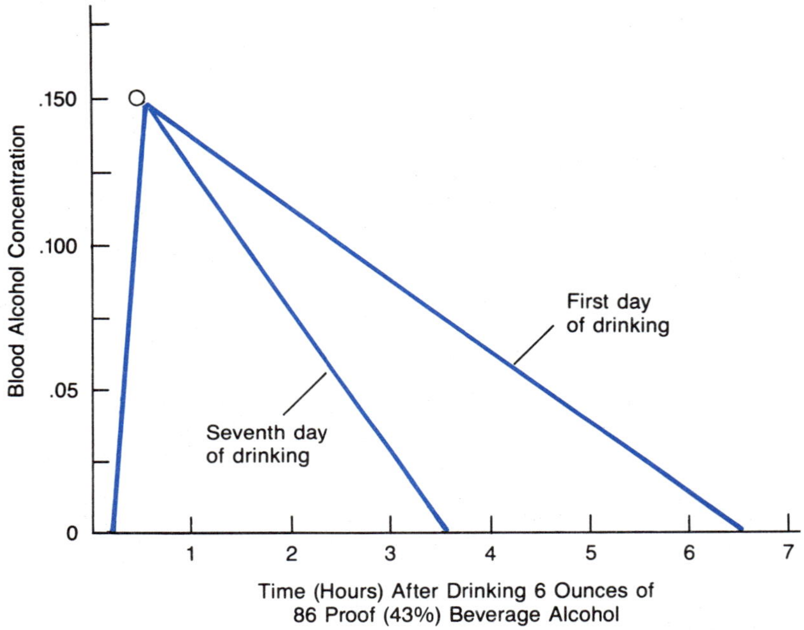

Source: J. Mendelson, *Alcohol: Use and Abuse in America* (Boston, MA: Little, Brown & Company, 1985), p. 175.

For reasons that are not yet entirely clear, prolonged drinking leads to metabolic tolerance. As this tolerance develops, the drinker must consume larger quantities of alcohol in order to achieve the desired effects.

THE ADAPTIVE AND MIDDLE STAGES OF ALCOHOLISM

Jellinek was the first authority on alcoholism to describe alcoholism as a progressive disease that moves through 3 stages, each of which is characterized by specific symptoms of physical and mental deterioration. (No one disputes the destruction alcohol abuse wreaks on the body, which we will be discussing below. The controversy rages over the *causes* and *treatment* of alcoholism, not on its effects on mind and body.)

In the first, or **adaptive, stage** the alcoholic is able to increase his or her intake gradually and still function normally. In fact, as his or her blood alcohol level rises, the drinker in the adaptive stage is likely to experience an increased level of performance in some areas. Only when his or her blood alcohol level begins to descend do the visible signs of drunkenness appear. Early in their drinking careers, most alcoholics unconsciously slip into "maintenance drinking"; that is, they learn how much alcohol they have to consume to keep their blood alcohol levels from falling below the point at which they are able to feel comfortable and function "normally."

Eventually, of course, reliance on alcohol becomes **dependence**, and alcoholics no longer have a choice as to whether they will drink or not. They cannot function without alcohol and have entered the **middle stage** of alcoholism, which is characterized by tolerance and **withdrawal**. Tolerance is a process whereby the body becomes accustomed to alcohol (or any other drug), and the user must use more and more of the substance involved to achieve the same effect he or she previously experienced at lower doses. In this phase of alcoholism, all the body's cells have become dependent on alcohol to function, and a drop in the BAC triggers a withdrawal syndrome, which begins immediately after the alcoholic stops drinking and lasts up to a few days.

In the early stages of alcoholism, withdrawal symptoms primarily include anxiety, agitation, nausea, headache, short-term memory and sleep disruptions, and tremors—the misery of the "hangover" even nonalcoholics experience after a bout of heavy drinking. As alcoholism progresses, however, withdrawal becomes a far more serious and painful matter. Typically, along with the physical wretchedness of the hangover, alcoholics experience remorse, guilt, shame, and self-loathing after they have drunk beyond their capacity. Severe symptoms of withdrawal include alcoholic **convulsions**, **hallucinations**, and **delirium tremens**.

Alcoholic convulsions are similar to grand mal epileptic seizures. They result from a number of different physical abnormalities, including low blood sugar level, hormonal imbalances, malnutrition, and the accumulation of toxins and waste products in the blood. Hallucinations, like the other symptoms of withdrawal, are signs of severe disruptions of the **central nervous system** brought on by the withdrawal of alcohol. Finally, delirium tremens, the most severe withdrawal symptom, includes hallucinations, mental confusion, trembling, convulsions, nausea, and irritability. Left untreated, it can be fatal.

Adaptive-stage alcoholism: The first stage of chronic alcoholism, during which the drinker is able to function normally despite his or her drinking problem.

Dependence: Reliance, either physical or psychological, on a psychoactive substance.

Middle-stage alcoholism: The second stage of chronic alcoholism, during which the drinker's body develops a tolerance for alcohol that requires the consumption of increasingly greater quantities to avoid the onset of withdrawal symptoms.

Withdrawal: The process the body goes through if denied a substance upon which it has become dependent.

Convulsions: Bodily contortions caused by violent involuntary muscle contractions, sometimes accompanied by loss of consciousness.

Hallucinations: Sensory perceptions not based on reality.

Delirium tremens (DTs): A psychotic reaction associated with chronic abuse of alcohol; symptoms include disorientation, hallucinations, intense fear, tremors, sweating, and fever.

Central nervous system: The brain and spinal cord.

The middle stage of alcoholism is also characterized by an increasing loss of control over the amount of alcohol consumed and by the phenomenon of craving. Craving is the intense, irresistible urge to drink, prompted at least in part by the body's demand that the level of alcohol to which it has adapted be maintained. Loss of control involves a growing inability to restrict drinking to socially appropriate occasions and locations. Out-of-control alcoholics frequently drink in the morning and throughout the day, hide bottles in their cars and throughout their houses, are frequently arrested for driving under the influence of alcohol, and carry alcohol in their briefcases or pocketbooks so that they never run the risk of not being able to get that next drink.

In this phase of alcoholism, the increasing need for alcohol is based on an effort to medicate the progressively punishing symptoms of withdrawal. The morning drink helps to quell feelings of extreme agitation, paranoia, the shakes, and headache. Past a certain point, however, alcohol no longer works as a mitigator of the problems it is causing. Alcoholics in this phase, however, will stop drinking only when they either pass out or become violently ill. Once a semblance of equilibrium returns, the drinking starts again and the downward spiral continues.

End-stage alcoholism: The final stage of chronic alcoholism, in which the drinker is usually socially and emotionally isolated and his or her physical health (and life) is at risk.

Malnutrition: An inadequate or unbalanced consumption of nutrients that produces negative effects on physical health.

Atrophy: Wasting away of bodily tissues.

Computerized tomography (CT): A technology that makes it possible to generate highly detailed cross-sectional images of the body; also known as computerized axial tomography (CAT).

Ventricles: Fluid-filled cavities in the center of the brain.

END-STAGE ALCOHOLISM

End-stage alcoholism involves the deterioration and eventual destruction of the central nervous system, the liver and other vital organs, and severe **malnutrition**. In the chronic alcoholic, the damage to the central nervous system is profound. This impairment is caused by a combination of the toxic effects of alcohol to the central nervous system and the nutritional deficiencies that accompany chronic alcoholism.

One effect of chronic alcoholism is a reduction in brain size. Shrinkage of the brain caused by **atrophy**, or wasting away, of the brain cells has been measured in many alcoholics. In the past, this shrinkage was discovered during autopsies. Today the effects of alcohol abuse on the brain can be measured by sophisticated technological devices, such as **computerized tomography (CT)** scans that give X-ray–like pictures of the brain.

One measure of shrinkage is the size of the **ventricles**, the fluid-filled cavities in the central part of the brain under the cerebral cortex. Several studies have shown an increase in the ventricle size in advanced stage alcoholics. [2] Another measure

FIGURE 4.2
Effect of Alcohol on Brain Size

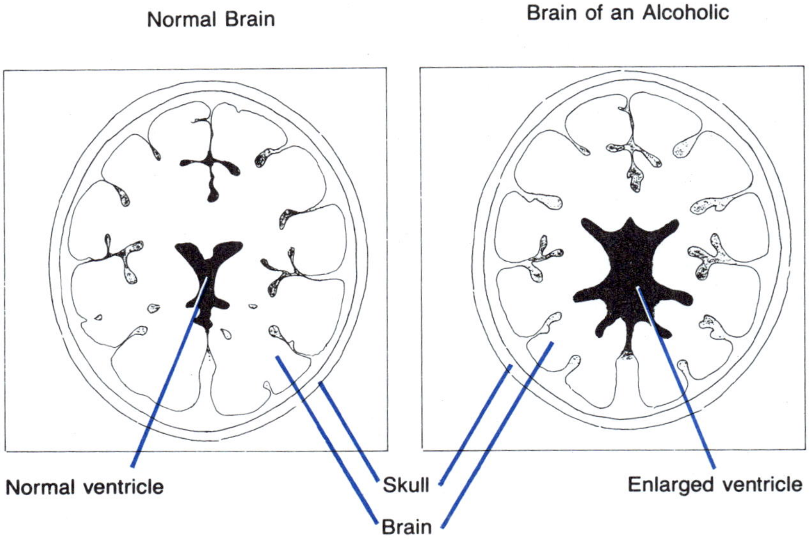

This illustration of a computerized tomography (CT) scan of the brain shows that chronic alcoholism can cause the ventricles (fluid-filled cavities) to enlarge and the brain to shrink.

of brain atrophy is the size of the **sulci**, the valleys on the surface of the cortex. Wider sulci are an indication of brain atrophy and are often found in cases of end-stage alcoholism and senility.

Brain atrophy results in the loss of some mental capabilities, including impairment of the skills involved in problem solving, abstract reasoning, and eye-hand coordination. But alcohol itself is only secondarily responsible for some of these effects. A great deal of the impairment experienced by heavy drinkers results from the vitamin deficiencies associated with extremely poor eating habits. Also, alcoholics are vulnerable to a number of infections and frequently experience head injuries in repeated falls. Yet there is evidence that alcohol in itself contributes to brain damage. For example, there is evidence that social drinkers

Sulci: Valleys or fissures on the surface of the brain.

Did You Know That . . .

Delirium tremens (DTs), the most extreme manifestation of alcohol withdrawal, can stress the system so greatly as to cause death in one out of every four cases.

experience the same type of memory losses that alcoholics do, but they are less severe in nature. Moreover, there is a correlation between the memory losses and the amount of alcohol consumed. [3] The less frequently someone drinks, the less vulnerable he or she is to alcohol-related memory impairment.

There is no doubt that in end-stage alcoholism the combination of the toxic effects of alcohol on the central nervous system and the nutritional deficiencies that accompany chronic alcoholism frequently result in profound cerebral dysfunction. **Korsakoff's syndrome**, also known as Korsakoff's psychosis, is a form of brain damage that most typically accompanies chronic alcoholism. It is characterized by extreme confusion and impairment of memory, especially of recent events, while other intellectual functions remain relatively intact. The alcoholic afflicted by this syndrome often compensates for his or her inability to remember current events and facts by making up stories. This process of fabrication is known as **confabulation**.

Wernicke's syndrome, also known as Wernicke's encephalopathy, is the result of **thiamine** deficiency. Thiamine, a B vitamin, is essential to the proper functioning of the central nervous system. Most alcoholics also suffer from malnutrition, and thiamine is consequently lacking in their diets. Wernicke's syndrome is characterized by paralysis of normal eye movements, problems with walking, and disordered thinking. Wernicke's syndrome is often seen in combination with Korsakoff's syndrome and in these cases is referred to as Wernicke-Korsakoff's syndrome.

Korsakoff's syndrome: A particularly dramatic form of amnesia associated with chronic alcohol abuse in which the individual is unable to recall virtually any of his or her recent or remote past; victims often attempt to cope by "recalling" events that never happened (confabulating).

Confabulation: Fabrication invented by an alcoholic who can't remember actual events.

Wernicke's syndrome: A condition characterized by paralysis of normal eye movements, problems with walking, and disordered thinking.

Thiamine (B_1): A B-complex vitamin found in green vegetables and other foods that is essential to the proper functioning of the nervous, digestive, and circulatory systems.

ALCOHOL ABUSE AND THE LIVER

As we saw in chapter 2, the liver works heroically to break alcohol down into harmless substances and subsequently to eliminate it from the body. As we also learned, the liver's enzymes first break alcohol down into acetaldehyde, which is in turn oxidized into acetate in the liver. Too much acetaldehyde in the body, however, makes it more difficult for the liver to oxidize this still-toxic substance into acetate. This leads to the accumulation of acetaldehyde in the liver, which ultimately causes liver damage.

Alcohol abuse results in 3 diseases of the liver: fatty liver, alcoholic hepatitis, and cirrhosis. Among heavy drinkers, 90 to 100 percent show evidence of some features of fatty liver, an estimated 10 to 35 percent develop alcoholic hepatitis, and 10 to 20 percent develop cirrhosis. [4] In 1986, cirrhosis was the ninth leading cause of death in the United States. [5]

Fatty liver is the first stage of liver disease caused by alcohol. With abstinence, it is a potentially reversible accumulation of fat in the liver cells. Although this condition does not manifest itself in any particular set of symptoms, it does impair the liver's proper functioning. Fatty liver results both from an increase in the production of fatty acids and **triglycerides** (a kind of fat) by the liver and a decrease in the elimination of these products from the liver.

Alcoholic hepatitis is characterized by the inflammation and death of liver cells. Its symptoms include **jaundice**–a yellow discoloring of the skin and the whites of the eyes–and a feeling of general ill health. Usually, alcoholic hepatitis occurs after a serious drinking binge by an established alcoholic. Alcoholic hepatitis is also potentially reversible with abstinence.

Cirrhosis occurs when normal liver tissue is replaced by fibrous, or inflexible, tissue. Actually, the fibrous tissue is a kind of scar tissue that forms as healthy liver cells die off. Blood cannot flow normally through a cirrhotic liver; it backs up and the organ is gradually saturated with toxins. The flow of this poisoned blood to the brain results in the muddled thinking, impaired memory and judgment, and mental confusion that accompany cirrhosis.

As scar tissue continues to form in the liver, blood flow throughout the organ is reduced, causing the death of more liver cells. If the alcoholic continues to drink, the combination of fatty liver, alcoholic hepatitis, and cirrhosis has further harmful effects. As blood flow through the liver becomes more and more impaired, the pressure created causes the small blood vessels in the head, face, and chest to rupture, resulting in tiny, spiderlike patterns of broken blood vessels called spider angioma.

As cirrhosis progresses, blood vessels throughout the body continue to constrict, and blood must find alternate routes to the heart. One such route is through the thin-walled and delicate veins of the **esophagus**. The increased blood flow through these veins can cause them to dilate, rupture, and **hemorrhage**. End-stage alcoholics often vomit up blood, a sign that they are bleeding from their esophageal vessels, or **varices**. These hemorrhages are potentially fatal; in fact, bleeding from the esophageal varices is one of the major causes of death in cirrhosis.

Another potentially fatal effect of cirrhosis is its radical impairment of the liver's ability to metabolize toxins of any kind, which results in a dangerous buildup of poisons in the blood. This is particularly hazardous in the case of ammonia, which when present in excessive amounts in the blood can cause personality changes, lethargy, coma, and death.

Triglycerides: Fatty compounds found in foods and made in the body, consisting of a carbon "backbone" to which are attached three fatty acids.

Alcoholic hepatitis: An inflammation of the liver caused by excessive alcohol consumption; symptoms include lethargy, nausea, fever, and jaundice.

Jaundice: A yellow discoloring of the skin and eyes caused by the deposition of bile pigments.

Esophagus: A muscular tube situated between the larynx and stomach; it is essential to digestion.

Hemorrhage: Uncontrollable, excessive bleeding.

Varices: Abnormally dilated and misshapen blood vessels; plural of varix.

FIGURE 4.3
Alcohol and Liver Damage

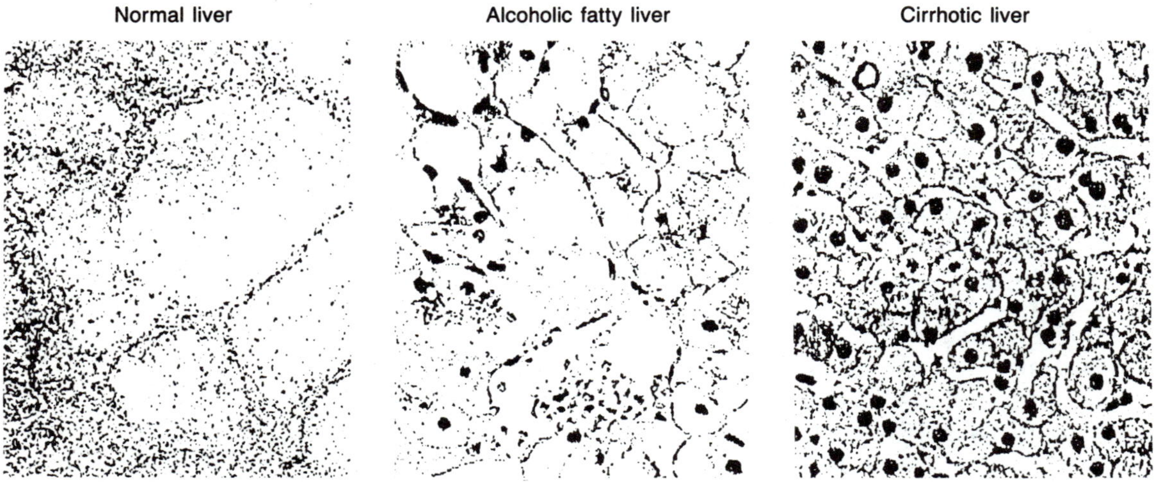

Source: Emanuel Rubin, M.D.

The liver suffers more from heavy alcohol use than any other organ in the body. Shown here is a section of a healthy liver that has a smooth, even texture, a section of a liver from an alcoholic patient that shows abnormal fat deposits, and a section of a cirrhotic liver that is covered with scar tissue.

As more and more healthy liver tissue is gradually replaced by fibrous tissue, the liver's production of essential chemical and hormonal substances radically slows. Reduced production of **prothrombin**, an ingredient essential to blood clotting, is one particularly dangerous side effect of cirrhosis. As prothrombin levels drop, the alcoholic may bruise easily and bleed excessively from small cuts and scrapes. He or she may also experience bleeding gums, frequent and severe nosebleeds, and bleeding under the skin. If the prothrombin level gets low enough, death from internal hemorrhaging can result.

Even with abstinence, cirrhosis is not reversible. However, up to a certain point, other major forms of liver damage are reversible if the alcoholic remains abstinent and receives proper nutritional therapy. If the alcoholic's drinking does not stop, death of the liver cells continues and the organ becomes irreparably clogged with dead cells and poisons. This radical impairment of liver function inevitably results in death.

Prothrombin: A protein found in the blood plasma that, when activated, is converted to thrombin, which in turn plays a major role in blood coagulation (clotting).

OTHER MEDICAL CONSEQUENCES OF ALCOHOLISM

Although the liver is by far the organ most seriously damaged by heavy drinking, virtually no system, region, or organ of the body is immune. Even moderate drinking disrupts the body, but, of course, this damage is usually quickly mended. However, the more one drinks, the more long-lasting and serious the consequences.

Although the connection between alcohol abuse and heart disease has been known for over a century, until very recently this was thought to be a result of malnutrition rather than the direct destructive effect of alcohol. However, a direct causative link between chronic, excessive alcohol consumption and heart disease has now been established, particularly in the case of the progressive disease that attacks the **mitochondria**, which are the energy-producing components of cardiac muscle cells. Without energy, the heart's pumping action fails over time, resulting in **alcoholic cardiomyopathy**, which is a degeneration of the heart muscle. This condition is generally seen in those who have been drinking abusively for 10 years or more, and its symptoms include shortness of breath and fatigue, chest pains, heart palpitations, and bloody **sputum** (a mixture of saliva and discharges from the respiratory system). Victims of alcoholic cardiomyopathy also suffer from **edema**, which results from a leakage of fluid from within blood vessels into the tissues of the arms, legs, face, abdomen, and lungs, causing swelling and difficulty in breathing. Experts believe that alcohol causes alcoholic cardiomyopathy because it inhibits the ability of cardiac muscle to contract.

The heart is a hollow, four-chambered organ that by rhythmic contraction forces the circulation of blood. Blood with low oxygen levels from the veins is pumped into the lungs, where it is reoxygenated, and then on to the arteries, which in turn supply the body with this reoxygenated blood. Apparently, alcohol damages the mitochondria in the heart muscle. Without energy, the heart's pumping action fails over time, resulting in all the symptoms of alcoholic cardiomyopathy. The prognosis of idiopathic (unexplained or spontaneous) cardiomyopathy is poor regardless of treatment, but alcoholic cardiomyopathy may have a good prognosis if marked reduction in alcohol use occurs. [6] Alcohol also disrupts the natural rhythms of the heart, causing **arrhythmia**. High blood pressure is also common among alcoholics and, if left untreated, is a contributor to heart failure.

(continued on p. 67)

Mitochondria: Small bodies, or organelles, found in living cells. They contain the enzymes used in metabolism; mitochondria are the "powerhouses" of the cell.

Alcoholic cardiomyopathy: A degenerative heart condition caused by excessive alcohol consumption.

Sputum: A mixture of saliva combined with mucous and other substances secreted by the lining of the respiratory tract.

Edema: An abnormal accumulation of fluid in the body.

Arrhythmia: Irregular heartbeat.

Did You Know That . . .

Drinking alcoholic beverages is known to raise blood pressure. If you choose to drink, experts recommend you lower the risks associated with high blood pressure, such as heart disease and stroke, by limiting your intake to 12 ounces of beer, 5 ounces of wine, or 1.5 ounces of 80-proof liquor per day.

Alcohol and Blood Pressure

People with high blood pressure and a fondness for margaritas can probably identify one potential hazard of this popular tequila drink: salt, traditionally applied to the rim of the glass. But there's another they might not recognize: alcohol.

A few years ago, the importance of alcohol as a cause of high blood pressure was not known. Current textbooks of medicine generally fail to mention the connection. But the new evidence is quite persuasive: imbibing more than a couple of drinks a day can raise blood pressure. Steady, heavy drinkers—those who consume 6 drinks (of beer, wine, or hard liquor) a day—are most conspicuously affected. But even people who consume about 3 drinks a day can measurably lower their blood pressure by going on the wagon for a week.

The evidence that alcohol plays a role in raising blood pressure initially came from epidemiologic investigations, which compared blood pressure in drinkers and nondrinkers. A 1986 study conducted at the Kaiser-Permanente health plan in California showed that alcohol contributes to raising blood pressure, independently of coffee or tea consumption, cigarette smoking, body weight, sex, race, or age.

These results confirm findings that have been turning up with some regularity since 1977, when an earlier Kaiser-Permanente study first drew attention to the relationship. Current estimates are that alcohol intake accounts for 5–25% of all cases of *primary* or *essential* **hypertension**—the sort that occurs without a detectable basis in some other disease.

Experimental studies now support these epidemiological observations. In a controlled study conducted in Jaipur, India, subjects with high blood pressure were asked to consume the equivalent of 6 drinks a day for 5 days; then they were put on the wagon for another 5. During the period of alcohol consumption, blood pressures gradually rose; when alcohol was stopped, pressures fell back to their starting values.

Australian researchers have shown that hypertensive men could lower their pressures if they cut their beer consumption from a six-pack a day to the equivalent of one regular beer a day; to do this, the subjects switched to a low-alcohol beer. The Australian subjects lost weight by reducing their beer consumption (no surprise), and the weight loss may also have helped lower blood pressure.

Why alcohol raises blood pressure is not clear. At least partly, the rise appears to be a reaction to alcohol withdrawal. This effect may be especially important in people who are alcohol dependent. But alcohol also directly raises blood pressure; the effect appears after less than a week of imbibing two or more drinks a day.

Consuming as much as a drink a day has little influence on blood pressure. The alcohol effect also appears to be reversible; heavy

Hypertension: The medical term for abnormally high blood pressure.

drinkers who quit typically lower their blood pressure by more than 10 points in both systolic (peak) and diastolic (trough) values.

A good case can be made that reducing alcohol consumption to no more than a drink a day is the first step to take after high blood pressure is diagnosed. There is no reason to think that alcohol, by "relaxing" the drinker, has any benefit whatever on blood pressure. . . .

Source: *Harvard Medical School Health Letter,* October 1987, pp. 1–2.

Cancers of the liver, **larynx**, **nasopharynx**, and esophagus occur more frequently in alcoholics than in the general population. [7] Chronic heavy drinking also causes inflammation of the lips and soft tissues of the mouth, as well as enlargement of a salivary gland called the parotid. It is believed that these effects are caused both by the direct tissue damage caused by alcohol and by the thiamine deficiency, mentioned earlier, from which many chronic alcoholics suffer because of their poor diets.

Both chronic and periodic excessive drinking can also cause damage to the structure of the small intestine. A small dose of alcohol has been shown to cause ulcerative **lesions** in the upper intestine. These lesions disappear once alcohol is removed.

The **pancreas**, another organ of the digestive system, is also vulnerable to alcohol abuse. The pancreas is responsible for producing and releasing a number of vital digestive enzymes, or substances necessary to break food down into materials the body can use for energy. Alcohol apparently irritates the pancreas, causing it to release abnormal levels of certain enzymes; this in turn inflames the pancreas. Eventually, the tissues of this organ break down and die, resulting in a condition called pancreatitis. This disease is extremely painful and can be fatal. Pancreatitis usually develops after 10 to 15 years of heavy drinking and is characterized by severe pain in the upper abdomen that sometimes radiates to the back and lower chest, nausea, vomiting, and constipation.

Another consequence of chronic heavy drinking is damage to muscle tissue that results in a condition called **alcoholic myopathy**, which is characterized by debilitating muscle fatigue. Although more than one-third of diagnosed alcoholics suffer from only mild myopathies, in some cases this malady can cause severe muscle cramps or weakness and episodes of myoglobinuria (dark-colored urine), thought to occur when the body tries to rid itself of myoglobin released by damaged muscle tissue. Acute alcoholic

(continued on p. 70)

Larynx: The upper part of the trachea; it contains the vocal cords.

Nasopharynx: The upper part of the oral cavity; it connects to the nasal passages.

Lesions: Localized, abnormal structural changes in any part of the body.

Pancreas: A soft, triangular-shaped gland that secretes a variety of digestive enzymes, including insulin, which regulates the body's metabolism of sugar.

Alcoholic myopathy: A degenerative muscle disorder associated with chronic alcoholism.

FIGURE 4.4
Health Effects of Chronic Alcohol Use

Brain: Because alcohol has a simple molecular structure, it easily passes through the protective blood/brain barrier. It depresses the portion of the brain that controls motor activity, impairs vision, and distorts emotions. End-stage alcoholism can cause brain atrophy, reduction in size of the brain, and permanent brain damage.

Skin: Alcohol dilates surface blood vessels, which causes a rush of blood to the skin. This makes the drinker feel warm but actually causes loss of body heat, which can lead to hypothermia in cold conditions.

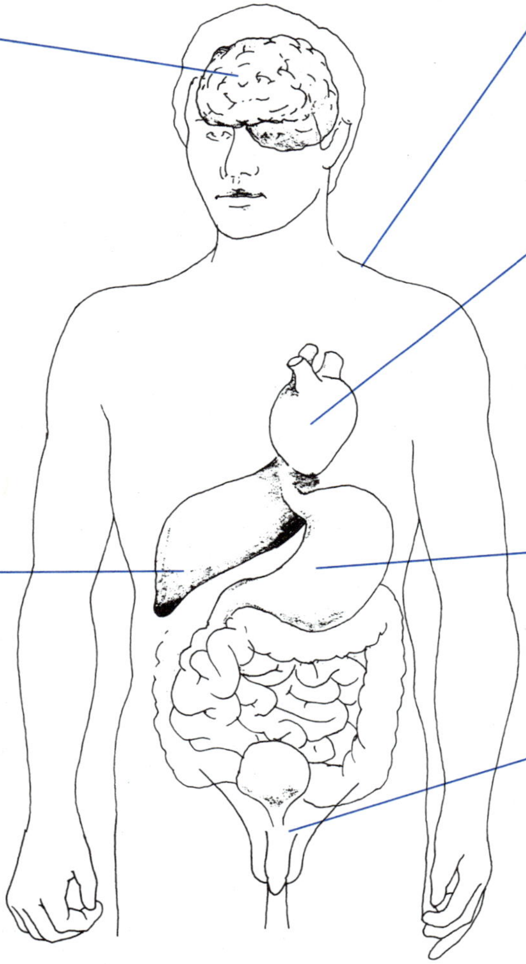

Heart: Alcohol affects the mitochondria, or the energy centers, of the cardiac muscle and can lead to alcoholic cardiomyopathy, or the deterioration of the heart muscle.

Liver: The liver is responsible for metabolizing alcohol, and can do so effectively when alcohol is consumed at a moderate level. When alcohol levels are excessive, the liver neglects its other vital functions, including the removal of other toxins from the body and the nutrition of the body's cells. Prolonged exposure to alcohol can cause fatty liver (a buildup of fat cells in the liver); alcoholic hepatitis (inflammation and death of liver cells); jaundice; and cirrhosis of the liver (replacement of normal liver cells with scar tissue).

Stomach: Alcohol stimulates the production of gastric juices. Large amounts of alcohol over an extended period of time can lead to ulcers, gastritis, and hematemesis (vomiting blood).

Reproductive system: The babies of pregnant women who consume alcohol can suffer fetal alcohol syndrome, an irreversible disorder that causes deformities, heart defects, and varying degrees of mental retardation. Alcohol also increases the risk of miscarriage. Men who drink heavily can experience episodes of impotence.

Long-term alcohol use damages many parts of the body. Some of the more serious health risks associated with alcohol use are described here.

Alcohol and Tobacco: A Deadly Duo

Cancer of the upper respiratory and alimentary tracts claimed over 23,000 lives in 1989 and 57,000 additional cases were diagnosed. The majority of individuals who fall prey to this type of cancer are males who abuse both alcohol and tobacco.

THE RISK

The fact that the risk of developing cancer of the esophagus, lip, tongue, mouth, pharynx or larynx, increases dramatically in people who are heavy users of alcohol and tobacco is substantiated by 30 years of collective research. Studies demonstrate that the risk to individuals dually addicted far outweighs the risk to individuals who abuse only one substance. This confirmed link between alcohol and tobacco abuse and an increased risk in upper alimentary and respiratory tract cancer makes this type of disease among the most preventable.

THE CORRELATION BETWEEN SMOKING AND DRINKING

It has been observed that individuals who drink alcohol have a greater tendency to smoke than non-drinkers. One of the first studies to establish and quantify the degree of association between drinking and smoking was reported in 1972. The investigation compared 130 alcoholic men hospitalized for alcohol withdrawal to 100 non-alcoholic psychiatric outpatients. Ninety-four percent of the alcoholic men smoked one or more packs of cigarettes per day, as compared to only 46 percent of the non-alcoholics, who smoked one or more packs per day.

Another study, which compared male and female alcoholics enrolled in an army drug and alcohol rehabilitation program to non-alcoholic army personnel and their relatives, affirmed the smoking-drinking association. The report found that individuals who were alcoholics smoked an average of 49 cigarettes per day, but that the non-alcoholic subjects smoked only 13 cigarettes per day. In addition, the study established a high correlation between the number of cigarettes smoked and the grams of alcohol consumed by alcoholics, as opposed to a very weak association for the non-alcoholic control group.

In a similar report, 58 percent of the non-drinkers were non-smokers, but the individuals who were alcoholics did not abstain from smoking. The finding that smokers who did not drink smoked significantly less than smokers who did drink was further substantiated in additional studies.

WHY DO MANY DRINKERS SMOKE MORE?

Studies released in the late 1950s, correlating heavy coffee consumption with smoking and drinking, suggested that a strong oral drive caused drinkers to smoke more frequently. However, new evidence suggests that a strong oral drive is not the culprit.

In one study, alcoholics who had successfully stopped drinking demonstrated no appreciable increase in smoking. In fact, some even smoked less with alcohol abstinence. If a strong oral drive was responsible for the drinking-smoking association, one would expect an increase in smoking during periods of alcohol abstinence.

An alternative theory claimed that drinkers smoked more due to social pressure. However, a study showing that alcoholics who drank alone smoked just as much as alcoholics who drink in the company of other people dispelled this theory. The most plausible explanation is that drinkers smoke more than non-drinkers due to a greater physiological need for nicotine.

Nicotine, the main psychoactive component of tobacco, is a potent chemical. It has a stimulating effect on the nervous system, causing, among other things, increased heart rate and mental stimulation. Once addicted to nicotine, a person may experience tremors of shakiness as blood levels of nicotine decrease to critically low levels. The smoker will crave another cigarette as blood levels reach this threshold to avoid these uncomfortable symptoms. Alcohol apparently causes blood levels of nicotine to fall more rapidly in smokers by activating enzymes in tissues which metabolize drugs. For example, rats pretreated with ethanol cleared nicotine from their blood more rapidly than rats not receiving ethanol. This research, coupled with numerous independent observations, strongly suggests that drinkers must smoke more in order to maintain the blood nicotine levels upon which they have become dependent.

WHY IS THERE MORE CANCER AMONG ALCOHOL AND TOBACCO USERS?

Investigations are under way to find an answer to this question. Laboratory studies have shown that alcohol enhances the metabolism of several tobacco associated carcinogens, including nitrosamines. It is known that tobacco and its smoke contain many classes of chemical carcinogens which must be activated to react with DNA and initiate steps towards carcinogenesis. Important in this activation process are cytochrome P-450 enzymes, which are induced by alcohol in heavy drinkers. Thus, alcohol and smoking are synergistic in increasing cancer risk.

Since alcohol increases the metabolism and hence the need for nicotine, it follows that the success of smoking cessation programs will be improved if drinking habits of patients are controlled. Treatment of incipient alcoholism thus becomes a prerequisite for the ultimate success of behavior modification aimed at the elimination of smoking.

—*Kristine Napier*

Source: Kristine Napier, *Priorities* (Spring 1990), pp. 6–7.

Chronic obstructive lung diseases (COLD): The current label for a class of respiratory infections, ranging from chronic but usually harmless disorders such as bronchitis to potentially fatal illnesses such as emphysema.

Anemia: A blood disorder characterized by a decrease in the number of red blood cells or in the amount of hemoglobin they contain; symptoms include fatigue, weakness, and pallor.

Fetal alcohol syndrome (FAS): A pattern of birth defects, cardiac abnormalities, and developmental retardation seen in babies of alcoholic mothers or mothers who abuse alcohol during pregnancy.

myopathies may cause sudden attacks of severe muscle pain or rapidly worsening cases of chronic myopathy.

Alcoholism can also result in a variety of lung diseases, including bacterial lung abscesses caused by vomiting and then aspirating, or inhaling, the stomach contents. **Chronic obstructive lung diseases**, such as emphysema and bronchitis, are common among alcoholics, particularly among male alcoholics who also smoke.

Among malnourished alcoholics, there is a high rate of pneumococcal pneumonia and tuberculosis. This is because malnutrition leads to a weakened immune system, making alcoholics vulnerable to many infectious diseases.

Alcoholics are prone to permanent kidney damage resulting from severe kidney infections; to **anemia**, or low red blood cell count, caused by deficiencies of iron and B vitamins; to hemoglobin deficiencies, which undermine the blood's ability to transport oxygen to the body's organs and tissues; and to lowered levels and impaired functioning of white blood cells, which are the components of blood responsible for fighting infection.

Finally, alcohol abuse poses a particular and horrendous danger to pregnant women because it can result in **fetal alcohol syndrome (FAS)**, a complex of physical and developmental de-

FIGURE 4.5
Blood Alcohol Transfer Between Mother and Fetus

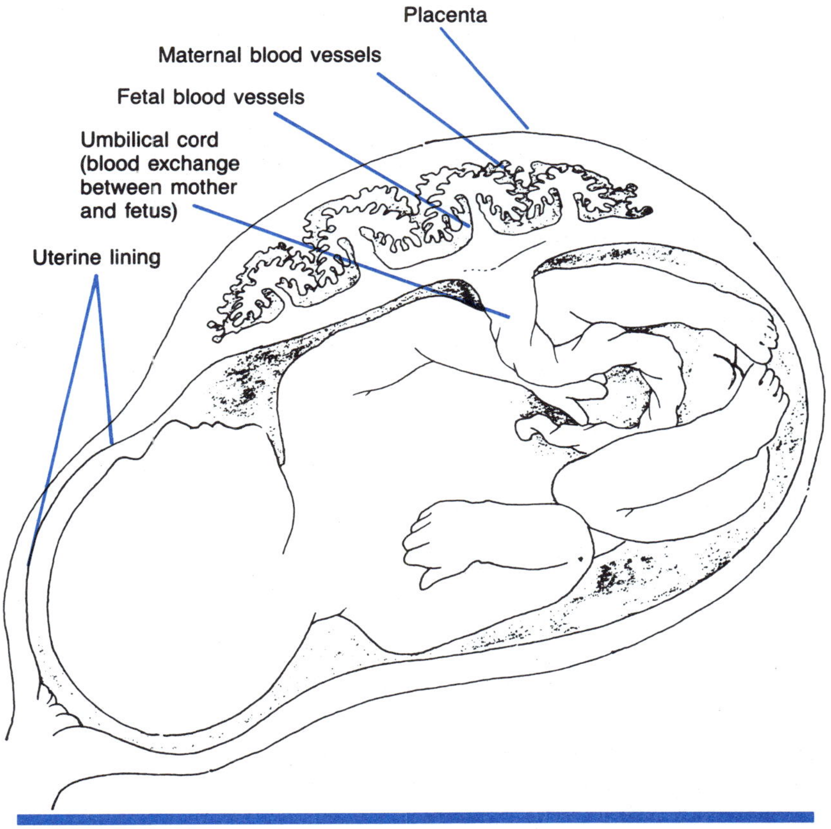

In an expectant mother, alcohol will freely cross the placenta and enter the developing fetus via the umbilical cord. Drinking during pregnancy can cause birth defects and is a major factor in mental retardation.

fects in children born to mothers who drink during pregnancy. The symptoms of fetal alcoholism include low birth weight, deformed facial features (flattened noses; small, abnormally wide-set eyes), possible cleft palate (holes in the roof of the mouth), heart defects, and possible central nervous system and spinal cord defects, which can range from sleep disturbances and **hyperactivity** to developmental delays and mental retardation.

FAS is seen with alarming frequency in the babies born to

Hyperactivity: A pattern of excessive activity, easy distractibility, and impulsiveness accompanied by a short attention span; it appears in early life and is more common in boys than in girls.

alcoholic mothers. Studies show that ethanol freely crosses the **placenta** and is directly toxic to the developing **fetus**. There is now evidence that pregnant women who have as little as a drink or two a day may have more miscarriages and deliver smaller babies who grow more slowly and have more behavioral difficulties than those of abstinent mothers. [8] Thus, it appears that *any* drinking by a pregnant woman may increase the risk of birth defects, and heavier drinking only exacerbates the problem. These facts argue that any woman who is actively attempting to become pregnant should consider abstaining from alcohol.

GENETICS AND PHYSIOLOGY

The hypothesis that alcoholism is a physically based disease has prompted intense and sophisticated research into possible genetic, biochemical, and physiological explanations as to its onset and progression. A seminal article on the genetic basis of alcoholism appeared in the April 18, 1990, issue of the *Journal of the American Medical Association.* The study was conducted by Kenneth Blum, a pharmacologist at the University of Texas Health Science Center in San Antonio, and Ernest Noble, a psychiatrist and biochemist at the UCLA Alcohol Research Center and a former director of the National Institute of Alcohol Abuse and Alcoholism (NIAAA). In the article, Blum and Noble discuss an analysis of genetic material from the brains of 70 cadavers, 35 of whom had died of alcoholism and 35 of whom were controls. [9] According to their findings, a genetic marker was found in 69 percent of the alcoholics but in only 20 percent of the nonalcoholics in the study. Blum and Noble concluded that a variant of a particular dopamine receptor could be linked directly with alcoholism. [10]

Other theories on the inheritability of alcoholism include the predication of an "alcoholic personality," or a set of inherited personality traits that predispose a minority of male alcohol abusers. This inherited personality theory has been promoted by Robert Cloninger, a psychiatrist who directs a research group at the School of Medicine at Washington University in St. Louis. [11]

Mark Schuckit, a psychiatrist at the University of California at San Diego Medical School, holds that alcoholics inherit an insensitivity to the effects of alcohol that prompts them to drink well beyond their capacity. [12] Schuckit's theory has been supported by another research team led by Barbara Lex of the Harvard Medical School. [13] Lex's research focused on a small number of women from alcoholic and nonalcoholic homes.

(continued on p. 76)

Placenta: The organ that develops in a woman's uterus during pregnancy that supplies the fetus with nourishment before its birth.

Fetus: A developing child from the eighth week of pregnancy to birth.

Alcoholism's Elusive Genes

Research into the genetics of alcoholism has taken off in the last 15 years, and with it has risen an air of inevitability. A dizzying array of data from around the world has led many people to think of this tragic disorder as a disease stemming from tainted genes.

This view received federal approval in 1985 with publication of a National Institute on Alcohol Abuse and Alcoholism (NIAAA) monograph titled "Alcoholism: An Inherited Disease." Recent research shows, according to the monograph, that heredity is a major contributing cause of alcoholism "in a larger proportion of cases, and perhaps in nearly all cases."

Scientists involved in the inheritance investigations are far more cautious in interpreting the findings, however, and some fear that NIAAA as well as many concerned individuals hold an oversimplified view of alcoholism's causes. Although these researchers search for genetic clues, they see alcoholism largely as a complex interaction of nature and nurture, with nature not necessarily being the dominant factor.

"It's easier to study the biology [of alcoholism]," says psychiatrist Marc A. Schuckit of the University of California at San Diego, who has identified several potential biological markers of alcoholism in the sons of alcoholics. "I know I'm only studying part of the pie, but there are no good environmental measures at this point."

Psychiatrist Donald W. Goodwin of the University of Kansas in Kansas City has found that children of alcoholics have an increased risk of becoming alcoholic even when brought up by adoptive parents, but he echoes Schuckit's caution. "The chances of a genetic factor playing an important role in some cases have increased sizably as a result of several adoption studies," he notes. "But these studies do not unequivocally prove that the major cause of alcoholism is genetic."

Psychologist John S. Searles of the University of Pennsylvania in Philadelphia goes a step further. Investigations of the genetic legacy in alcoholism have been "readily and uncritically accepted" by many scientists and clinicians, he maintains in the May [1988] *Journal of Abnormal Psychology.* Twin, adoption and biological-marker studies have also injected new vigor into the long-running, acrimonious debate over whether alcoholism is a disease or a learned behavior. But ironically, says Searles, that same work highlights the need to identify critical environmental pressures driving alcoholics to the bottle.

If investigators do not heed the environmental implications of genetic studies, he argues, it will hinder efforts to identify and treat alcohol abusers as early as possible.

A CASE IN POINT, says Searles, is an influential adoption study directed by psychiatrist C. Robert Cloninger of Washington University in St. Louis. Searles' reanalysis of the investigation suggests that as-yet-unspecified environmental pressures played a dominant role in determining alcohol abuse, not often-cited genetic factors.

Cloninger and his colleagues analyzed extensive government records in Sweden on 862 men and 913 women adopted at an early age, as well as background information on their biological and adoptive parents.

In 1981, they suggested there are two types of predisposition to alcoholism. Type 1, or "milieu-limited," alcoholism was found in three-quarters of the abusers. It occurred among men and women 25 years of age or older, and was linked to both a family history of alcoholism and four environmental influences: being reared by the biological mother for more than six months, greater age at the time of adoptive placement, more time spent in the hospital prior to placement and lower occupational status of the adoptive father. Less common was Type 2, or "male-limited," alcoholism. This brand was largely unaffected by the environment. It often developed during adolescence and was accompanied by aggressive behavior and law breaking.

According to Cloninger, Type 1s are often

highly anxious, emotionally dependent on others, shy and reflective. Type 2s, on the other hand, are impulsive, distractible and emotionally detached. Many alcohol abusers, he says, have some personality traits from both types.

Cloninger's discovery of two predictable types of alcoholism is "at best, preliminary and, at worst, unfounded," holds Searles. One problem with the Swedish study, he argues, was the lack of a nonadopted control group to test for the effects of being an adopted child. As in many adoption studies, Searles adds, it is not known whether biological mothers drank heavily during their pregnancies, possibly creating a constitutional (not genetic) risk for alcoholism in their unborn children. Furthermore, environmental measures were limited to what could be gleaned from official records and do not explore specific environmental influences on each adoptive child and his or her siblings.

To top it off, says Searles, alcohol abuse was defined in an unusual way—by the number of times each adoptee was registered with Sweden's county Temperance Boards for insobriety, usually after public intoxication, family violence or traffic offenses. There is no counterpart to this system in the United States.

In his review of Cloninger's data, Searles finds that almost half of the adoptees classified as alcohol abusers had neither a genetic predisposition nor an environmental "releaser" linked closely to their drinking habits. Overall, he concludes, unidentified environmental pressures were probably more important in determining alcohol abuse than were genetic factors.

There is also reason to question Goodwin's Danish adoption studies, maintains Searles. Goodwin and his co-workers found that adopted boys with an alcoholic biological parent are four times more likely to become alcoholic than are counterparts without an alcoholic biological parent. But nearly half the adoptive parents in the study had psychiatric disorders, Searles says, which may have influenced the development of alcoholism. It is also unclear, he says, why Goodwin's study found an increased genetic influence among subjects diagnosed as alcoholic, but not among those given milder diagnoses such as problem drinkers or heavy drinkers.

The adoption studies nevertheless indicate an important genetic predisposition to alcoholism in men and women with an extensive family history of alcohol abuse, Goodwin says. Cloninger's male-only Type 2 alcoholism is actually a co-ed category, adds Goodwin. Female alcoholics, he explains, are less likely to be diagnosed by physicians or arrested for criminal behavior, thus leading to an underestimate of their numbers.

AT THE LEAST, in Searles' view, adoption studies must move beyond a reliance on government records to diagnose alcohol abuse. Some investigations, he says, have inaccurately lumped "problem drinkers" and "heavy drinkers" into the alcoholic category.

A better picture of genetic and environmental contributions to alcoholism, says Searles, may come from the Colorado Adoption Project, an extensive study incorporating measures of environmental influences on each sibling in an adopted child's family. This long-term investigation of 182 adopted infants and 165 control infants was launched in 1975 by psychologist Robert Plomin and his colleagues of the University of Colorado in Boulder; the children are still too young to be evaluated for alcoholism and alcohol abuse.

Another approach in determining the development of alcoholism involves tracking a large group over several decades. For example, in an analysis of a prospective 40-year study of 600 men begun in the 1940s by Harvard researchers, psychiatrist George Vaillant of Dartmouth University in Hanover, N.H., concluded in 1983 that the major risks for alcoholism were having an alcoholic parent and coming from an ethnic background that condones adult drunkenness. Antisocial behavior and emotional problems such as depression are usually the result of alcoholism, he reported, not its cause.

But several researchers, including psychologist Robert A. Zucker of Michigan State University in East Lansing, have reanalyzed Vaillant's data and found that adolescent antisocial behavior, including misbehavior at school and truancy, played an important role in stimulating later alcoholism. Moreover, critics charge that since Vaillant's study began when participants were teenagers, it neglected childhood influences on adult alcoholism.

In an effort to identify people with a genetic vulnerability to alcoholism, investigators have sought biological markers appearing exclusively among youngsters with a family history of alcohol dependence. Schuckit has reported that, compared with sons of nonalcoholics, sons of alcoholics feel less drunk, display a less intense hormonal reaction and exhibit less body sway after drinking [*Science News:* 11/21/87]. In addition, sons of alcoholics have a distinctive brainwave pattern also found among abstinent alcoholics.

Children in these marker studies are being followed into adulthood, and researchers are attempting to chart important events and influences in their lives that might contribute to alcohol dependence.

ON THE MOLECULAR LEVEL, scientists at the NIAAA are looking for associations between specific markers on DNA and drinking patterns among members of families with a history of alcoholism. Experiments with mice bred to prefer alcohol over water have revealed a potential gene position on chromosome 1 possibly involved in the control of alcohol intake. The function of the protein coded at the gene position is unknown.

These and other biological-marker studies are just beginning, says Schuckit. It remains to be seen if any biological markers exist in women or across ethnic groups, and how biological mechanisms responsible for reactions to alcohol might affect the development of alcoholism.

"It's clear from family history studies on alcoholism that something in addition to genetic transmission is going on," says psychiatrist and alcoholism researcher Theodore Reich of the Jewish Hospital of St. Louis. "That 'something' is a potent phenomenon."

He and his colleagues are developing measures of the extent to which youngsters resemble their alcoholic parents and their siblings in various behavioral and psychological characteristics. If siblings develop increasingly different susceptibilities to alcoholism as they age, says Reich, "the effect of aging on susceptibility is likely to be culturally based. Genetic effects are usually more stable."

Biologically inherited factors still may influence the transmission of alcoholism, notes Reich. Several genetic mechanisms, for instance, may be related to the process of becoming addicted to a variety of drugs. On the other hand, some people may inherit buffers to alcohol use. One such buffer is a genetically based enzyme deficiency found among many Asians that delays alcohol metabolism and causes facial flushing, queasiness and other unpleasant physiological reactions after ingestion of small amounts of alcohol.

Psychiatric disorders with a genetic legacy also may lead to alcoholism, Reich says. Alcoholics often have other psychiatric diagnoses, including antisocial personality (marked by rebelliousness, family and social problems and law breaking), anxiety, depression and schizophrenia.

For now, though, a direct connection between heredity and alcoholism is a "missing link," says anthropologist Dwight B. Heath of Brown University in Providence, R.I. The question of who is at risk is a sticky one, notes Heath, who studies cultural and social influences on alcohol use. It may be true, he explains, that half of hospitalized alcoholics have alcoholic relatives and one out of four sons of alcoholics become alcoholics themselves, but this says nothing about any individual's risk of alcoholism.

"Certainly there are more sons of alcoholics who do not have drinking problems than who do, just as there are many problem drinkers who have no alcoholic relatives," says Heath. "No one is genetically predestined to become an alcoholic. Even if the genetic missing link were eventually found, the interaction of various environmental factors is certainly crucial if alcoholism is to occur in an individual."

A problem of definition

Epidemiologists estimate there are about 10 million severe alcoholics and another 7 million alcohol abusers in the United States. At the extremes, alcohol abuse is easy to identify, but the distinction between heavy drinking and alcoholism is often murky.

The National Council on Alcoholism defines alcoholism as a "chronic, progressive and potentially fatal disease" marked by "repeated drinking that causes trouble in the drinker's personal, professional or family life. When they drink, alcoholics can't always predict when they'll stop, how much they'll drink or what the consequences of their drinking will be."

The recently revised manual of psychiatric disorders published by the American Psychiatric Association describes three patterns of alcohol abuse or dependence: regular daily drinking of large amounts, regular heavy drinking limited to weekends, and long periods of sobriety punctuated by heavy drinking binges lasting for weeks or months. "It is a mistake to associate one of these particular patterns exclusively with alcoholism," advises the manual.

The abuse of other drugs, including marijuana, cocaine, heroin, amphetamines and sedatives, often accompanies alcohol dependence, according to the manual.

However alcoholism is defined, it is clear that most alcohol is consumed by a small percentage of people. In the United States, 10 percent of the drinkers imbibe 50 percent of all alcohol consumed.

—B. Bower

Source: Bruce Bower, *Science News*, Vol. 134 (30 July 1988), pp. 74–75, 79.

Schuckit has also presented another theory on the physiological basis of alcoholism that maintains that alcoholics inherit a flaw in the way they metabolize alcohol. According to this theory, alcohol is not broken down properly in the livers of alcoholics, resulting in an abnormal buildup of acetaldehyde, one of the products of alcohol's oxidization. In the March 1976 issue of *Scientific American,* Charles Lieber, then chief of the research program on liver disease at the Bronx Veterans Administration Hospital, reported that the same amount of alcohol produced very different blood acetaldehyde levels in alcoholics and nonalcoholics. Lieber theorized that the abnormal buildup of acetaldehyde was caused in part by a malfunctioning of the liver's enzymes. [14]

In *Under the Influence,* a widely read book by James Milam and Katherine Ketcham published in 1981, the authors took up the acetaldehyde hypothesis, claiming that the abnormal buildup of this metabolite is a primary biological and genetic basis for alcoholism, which they claimed is completely biologically determined. Milam and Ketcham also took this hypothesis one step further, maintaining that a buildup of acetaldehyde in the brain radically disrupts the work of the neurotransmitters, competing with brain enzymes and thereby interfering with their vital work in regulating neurotransmitter activity. According to Milam and Ketcham, the acetaldehyde that builds up in the brain interacts with certain neurotransmitters to create tetrahydroisoquinolines (TIQs), chemical agents that the authors hold responsible for the intense craving for alcohol that heavy drinkers experience. [15]

Did You Know That . . .

Doctors no longer recommend alcohol as a sedative because it can become addictive and actually disrupt sleep.

PSYCHOLOGY AND BEHAVIOR

Although the disease theory of alcoholism has won wide acceptance among alcoholism therapists and the general public alike, there is a strong body of opinion that disputes both the inheritability of alcoholism and its biological basis as well. For example, writing in the August 1990 issue of *The Atlantic Monthly,* Stanton Peele, a leading theorist in the field of alcohol abuse, disputes the validity of much of the genetic findings, claiming that no real scientific link has been established between genetic idiosyncrasies and subsequent drinking behavior. He writes:

> Addictive drinking is one of a range of dependencies that people may acquire in attempting artificially to regulate their sense of themselves and their world. Some people become compulsively enmeshed in destructive drinking as they pursue sensations that they are progressively less able to attain through any other means. And yet we cannot take the power and the seeming inevitability of this self-destructiveness for proof that it is written in the genes. [16]

Peele presents several theories on the causation of alcohol abuse that involve sociological and psychological explanations. One such theory has to do with the expectations a person brings to his or her drinking experiences. If someone has become convinced that alcohol will make him or her more attractive, gregarious, relaxed, sociable, or whatever, this is the effect he or she will feel alcohol induces even when all the evidence is to the contrary. According to this theory, one factor that distinguishes alcoholics from normal drinkers is precisely the fact that they have stronger expectations about how alcohol will affect them. Peele cites research done by Mark Goldman, a psychologist at the University of South Florida. He and his colleagues have claimed to demonstrate that future problem drinkers could be diagnosed during their adolescent years on the basis of their expectations about alcohol, even before they had begun drinking. [17] These beliefs and assumptions about alcohol tend to be based on parental, peer group, and cultural influences and have nothing to do with physiology.

Another theory that contravenes the disease concept of alcoholism involves learned cultural attitudes toward drunkenness and "out-of-control" behavior in general. For instance, Chinese Americans and Jewish Americans have traditionally experienced very low rates of alcoholism. In both these sub-groups, excessive drinking is viewed as a psychological dependence and a sign of weakness, as character flaws that should be neither tolerated nor indulged. Native Americans and Irish Americans, on the other hand, tend to view alcohol as an almost magically powerful potion over which they have no control. In sum, Peele says, "people from social backgrounds in which antisocial drunkenness is strongly disapproved of and people who believe they *can* and *should* control their drinking are less likely to lose themselves in the experience of intoxication." [18]

Bolstering the claims of those who reject the disease concept is the fact that it does not take into account those alcoholics who do not progress through the usual stages or do not develop the disease characteristics described by Jellinek. Neither does the disease concept accommodate those alcoholics who are able to reduce the amount they drink to the point where their drinking does not make their lives unmanageable. Moreover, it fails to explain why some alcoholics are able to give up drinking spontaneously and completely.

Of course, as we mentioned earlier, proponents of the disease concept would simply say that those who drink for psychological reasons, who are able to moderate the amount they drink or to quit "cold turkey" with no disastrous withdrawal symptoms, may in fact have problems with alcohol but cannot be classified as alcoholics. Be that as it may, there is general agreement that once physical *or* psychological dependence on alcohol has been established, such drinkers can almost never return to "normal" drinking and can reenter the mainstream of life only through total abstinence maintained by some form of **rehabilitation** and counseling. In the next chapter, we will review various treatment methods available to the alcoholic and his or her family.

Rehabilitation: The process of recovering from a disease such as alcoholism.

CHAPTER 5

Getting Help

THROUGHOUT MOST OF HISTORY, little effort was made either to understand or to treat alcoholism. The object of pity or scorn, the desperately ill alcoholic was left pretty much to fend for himself or herself, the unaided victim of the physical and mental deterioration we discussed in the previous chapter.

THE HISTORICAL PERSPECTIVE

In 1804, however, Dr. Thomas Trotter, an Edinburgh physician, published a now classic treatise on alcoholism that presented the first scientific consideration of alcoholism on record. Entitled "An Essay, Medical, Philosophical, and Chemical, on Drunkenness and its Effects on the Body," Trotter's work came to the then-revolutionary conclusion that

> in the writings of medicine, we find drunkenness only cursorily mentioned among the powers that injure health. . . . The priesthood hath poured forth its anathemas from the pulpit; and the moralist, no less severe, hath declaimed against it as a vice degrading to our nature. . . . In medical language, I consider drunkenness, strictly speaking, to be a disease, produced by a remote cause, and giving birth to actions and movements in the living body that disorder the functions of health. [1]

For the most part, Trotter's work was either derided or ignored. However, similar efforts to move alcoholism from the moral and religious arena to the field of science and medicine

FIGURE 5.1
Treatment for Alcohol Abuse in the Nineteenth Century

Source: Rutgers Center of Alcohol Studies.

During the mid- and late-nineteenth century, some doctors began treating alcoholism as a medical illness, and hospitals and treatment centers such as the one pictured here began to be established. The Women's National Hospital was built in the 1870s in Wilton, Connecticut, for the express purpose of treating alcoholic and drug-dependent women.

were also being made in the United States at the time his essay appeared. Writing in the United States contemporaneously with Trotter, Dr. Benjamin Rush recognized drunkenness as an illness. During the 1830s, the medical superintendent of Worcester, Massachusetts, Dr. Samuel Woodward, and Dr. Eli Todd were forming small groups that sought to help "intemperate persons" by hospitalizing them rather than banishing them to jails or workhouses. This was significant because for the first time alcoholics were not treated the same way as criminals, the indigent, or the insane.

Between 1841 and 1874, this movement was responsible for the establishment of 11 nonprofit hospitals and houses for the treatment of alcoholics. Founded in 1876, the *Journal of Inebriety* advanced the views and findings of those who had come to believe that alcoholism was a medical illness that could be diagnosed and treated as such. Unfortunately, this view met with widespread criticism from both the religious and legal communities, and before Prohibition was enacted, the *Journal* had folded and all the hospitals had been closed.

The Washington Temperance Society, founded in 1840, marked another milestone in the journey toward an enlightened understanding of alcohol abuse. In many ways, the Washington Temperance Society resembled all the other temperance groups that flourished during the mid-nineteenth century. Fueled by religious zeal, it sought to help "drunkards" achieve sobriety and salvation through complete abstinence. What makes the Washington Temperance Society stand out, however, is that it was founded by 6 reformed alcoholics who declared: "Drunkard! Come up here! You can reform! We don't slight the drunkard! We love him!" [2] The organizing principle of this society was that one drunkard would help another and that each would maintain his sobriety by recounting his experiences with alcohol and subsequent "rescue" in public. At the height of its success in 1844, the Washington Society numbered 100,000 "reformed common drunkards" and 300,000 "common **tipplers**." [3] Similar in many ways to Alcoholics Anonymous, the Washington Society was based on the principle of **self-help** and organized around regular meetings, sharing experiences, fellowship, reliance on God, and total abstinence. Unfortunately, controversy and in-fighting quickly consumed this group, and it ceased to exist as an organization independent of the temperance movement as a whole by 1848.

Not until the 1930s did any major effort to view the alcoholic as the victim of an illness reemerge. In 1935, the New York stockbroker Bill Wilson and the Ohio physician Bob Smith cofounded Alcoholics Anonymous. At about the same time, a group of scientists gathered at Yale University to found the *Quarterly Journal of Studies on Alcohol (QJSA)*. Unlike the *Journal of Inebriety*, the *QJSA* achieved respectability in the scientific community and became a clearinghouse for solid information on alcoholism. The founders of this journal, Yandell Henderson, Howard Haggard, Leon Greenberg, and E. M. Jellinek, are recognized as pioneers in the modern understanding of alcoholism. Haggard published seminal findings on the metabolism of alcohol in the *QJSA*, and Jellinek's classic *The Disease Concept of Alcohol-*

Tippler: Colloquial term used to describe one who drinks intoxicating beverages, especially to excess.

Self-help: Label applied to treatment programs in which lay people rather than professionals are the primary source of assistance and support.

ism was also published while he was at Yale. Other important advances grew out of the Yale experience: The Yale Center of Alcohol Studies and the Classified Abstract Archive of Alcohol Literature were established. The Yale Plan Clinic was also set up to diagnose and treat alcoholism. The Yale Summer School of Alcohol Studies, now the Rutgers School, educated professionals and laypeople. Yale's far-reaching influence also resulted in the founding of the volunteer National Council on Alcoholism in 1944. Designed to provide information and education on alcohol and alcoholism to the general public, the council was established by Jellinek and Marty Mann, herself a recovered alcoholic. She became the Council's first president.

TREATMENT TODAY

Despite the fact that the medical and psychiatric establishment has grown by leaps and bounds in its understanding of the complex and bewildering condition known as alcoholism, effective treatment continues to be elusive. To be sure, at the end of the twentieth century there is a proliferation of treatments, including public and private facilities, long- and short-term approaches, **inpatient programs** and **outpatient programs** that rely to various degrees on the guidelines established by Alcoholics Anonymous, and so forth. However, addictions of all sorts are by their nature tenacious and intractable, and this very fact dogs every effort to establish full physical, mental, and spiritual recovery from alcoholism.

Although there is talk from time to time about teaching alcoholics to drink "normally," most experts in the field of alcoholism, as well as most recovering alcoholics themselves, insist that total, permanent abstinence is the essential first goal of successful treatment. Whether psychological problems *result* from alcoholic drinking or *cause* it is a vexed question that may never be answered, but it is agreed that the psychic distress associated with alcoholism cannot begin to be alleviated until the victim clears his or her system of alcohol and keeps it cleared.

Recovering alcoholics themselves, as well as professionals in the field of the treatment of alcoholism, agree that getting the problem drinker to admit that he or she has a problem is the first and probably the biggest hurdle on the path to recovery. Alcoholics can literally drink themselves to death before admitting that their drinking is causing them grievous mental and bodily harm. This refusal on the part of alcoholics to admit that they are

Inpatient programs: Alcohol treatment programs usually offered at clinics or hospitals that require the patient to remain on the premises for a given period of time.

Outpatient programs: Alcohol treatment programs that allow the patient to live at home during the rehabilitation process.

FIGURE 5.2
Advertising Campaigns

Source: Reader's Digest Foundation, National Institute on Alcohol Abuse and Alcoholism.

Many advertising campaigns sponsored by public and private organizations try to reach the problem drinker and encourage him or her to seek help.

in trouble with alcohol is called "denial," and it keeps many problem drinkers from seeking help. Denial is also responsible for relapses once recovery has begun.

Many alcoholics *do* recognize the need to stop drinking, however, and voluntarily reach out for treatment. In some cases it is necessary for family members to arrange for a professionally managed **intervention** in which the alcoholic is confronted di-

(continued on p. 87)

Intervention: A procedure in which friends or members of a substance abuser's family, usually working with the assistance of a professional therapist, directly confront the abuser at a prearranged time and place in an attempt to persuade him or her to seek immediate treatment.

Help for Those Who Drink Too Much

First came his arrest for drunk driving, which made the local papers and television. Then he confronted the chilling reality of being passed over for promotion; and finally, an ultimatum from the boss: Either seek help for alcoholism or be fired. After years of drinking uncontrollably, Tom, badly frightened, finally checked into an alcoholism treatment center.

Earlier he had sought help from Alcoholics Anonymous, which didn't work for him. This time an advertisement for Parkview-Westchester in Yorktown Heights, N.Y., suggested an approach that appealed to him. Following an evaluation by the center's professional staff, Tom, a police officer, began a 30-day period of intensive treatment in which he learned how alcoholism was not only destroying his life but also wrecking the lives of those around him.

Parkview, a freestanding residential rehabilitation center, enrolls clients who agree to spend about a month living at the center while undergoing intensive treatment for their alcoholism.

Tom began each day at 7 A.M. with breakfast, followed by a group meeting with other patients, whose influence ultimately turned out to be crucial to his recovery. "We all denied our alcoholism at first," Tom says, "but then we came to admit it, which is the first step in recovery."

Afternoons spent with therapists helped convince him that his drinking problem was a disease for which abstinence was the only control. Evening visits by volunteers from AA reinforced the lessons of the day. Along the way, Tom's wife and daughter spent a week in a separate wing of Parkview, which stresses the importance of educating other family members about the nature of alcoholism. The program gave Tom the discipline he had been unable to develop himself.

Fortunately for Tom, most of the . . . cost of treatment was covered by insurance. A year later he has not touched a drop.

For 32-year-old Jack, a similar career of misery ended in a Washington, D.C., clinic. By age 17 he was abusing alcohol, but outright dependence didn't show up until his mid twenties. He vainly tried nearly anything, including AA, to help him stop. The light dawned when Jack seriously injured himself falling from his car while drunk. He decided to go to Seton House, an alcohol recovery center at Providence Hospital. "Therapists there convinced me I had a chemical dependence that would eventually kill me unless I gave it up," Jack recalls.

After years of addiction, he accepted the discipline and structure of the 28-day, hospital-based residential treatment program with its 90-day follow-up. He returned to college to finish work on a long-neglected undergraduate degree and now works as a counselor to other alcoholics at Seton House.

Not all stories of recovery are so dramatic. Nor does every alcoholic need such extreme treatment. But the cases show how even advanced alcoholism can be brought under control if the victim finds appropriate therapy and is able to take advantage of it in time. The tragedy is that a vast majority of the country's nearly 15 million alcoholics deny that they have a problem, fail to recognize the seriousness of their dependency until it's too late or resist offers of help because they believe all is lost. It needn't be that way.

Early signs of trouble

Alcoholism can't be cured, but it can be arrested and its victims restored to a more normal life. Budding alcoholism can be detected and interrupted before it reaches a severe stage. Early signs of trouble, though, are more likely to be picked up by family, friends or the boss than by a doctor.

If there is a true "alcoholic personality," researchers have been unable to settle on a consistent definition. Many authorities depict the alcoholic as depressed, insecure, compulsive, tense or fearful, and burdened with a sense of guilt and isolation. Because drink seems to blunt fear and anxiety and impart a feeling of confidence and acceptance, the theory goes, the drinker tends to use alcohol increasingly as a defense and to depend on it for fabricated esteem. Over time it takes more and more alcohol to achieve the effect.

However, those theories are based on observations of alcoholics already deeply in trouble. When several large groups of men were studied prospectively (that is, before and after they became addicted) over a period of 40 years, Harvard alcoholism authority George Vaillant writes in *The Natural History of Alcoholism,* personality quirks more often appeared to have been the result rather than the cause of alcoholism.

So-called problem drinking doesn't always progress to the worst stages of alcoholism. More telling is a person's compulsion for alcohol, increasing dependency on its effects and a gradual advance from occasional to frequent drinking. Most authorities agree that alcoholism is a complex disorder that is influenced by a combination of physiological, psychological and environmental factors. Says the National Council on Alcoholism: "The person with alcoholism cannot consistently predict on any drinking occasion the duration of the episode or the quantity that will be consumed."

The search for treatment

Faced with an incurable disease, alcoholics have only one reliable way of bringing the disease under control: swearing off alcohol for good. Most therapists believe the evidence is too shaky to justify adopting moderate drinking habits as a general goal of treatment. These are the main techniques currently used to treat alcoholism:

Inpatient treatment. No matter where the treatment is sought, an alcoholic who is intoxicated will probably receive medical care in the form of hospitalization and steps to eliminate alcohol from the blood. If, after the patient is detoxified, the decision is for hospital rehabilitation, antidepressants and vitamin supplements may be prescribed to overcome withdrawal symptoms and malnutrition. Personnel will continuously monitor vital signs. According to Boston University's Dr. Leonard Saxe, who has analyzed the cost and effectiveness of alcoholism treatment for the federal government's Office of Technology Assessment, alcoholics admitted to a hospital program (which lasts three or four weeks) usually have relatively stable social backgrounds and fewer years of hard drinking behind them.

Private psychiatric hospitals also treat a sizable number of people who abuse alcohol, although alcoholism might not be the primary diagnosis. Treatment in a psychiatric facility is likely to include individual and group therapy, alcohol education and sometimes the use of Antabuse, a drug that makes you sick if you try to drink alcohol after taking it.

Inpatient treatment is also available at freestanding clinics associated with a hospital, like Seton House, or in facilities like Parkview that are not part of a hospital. Freestanding residential rehabilitation typically consists of group counseling, in which a leader conducts sessions that try to change the pattern of the drinker's behavior or get at the root cause. Family involvement is often crucial, as is the association with self-help groups like AA, and the fellowship of men and women who help each other stay sober by sharing their experiences and encouraging each other to remember that "we are powerless over alcohol.". . .

Outpatient therapy. Probably about 90% of the one million alcoholics under treatment each year are in outpatient therapy. They spend part of the day in a hospital or residential clinic and return home at night. Both hospitals and freestanding centers offer outpatient therapy, which generally resembles inpatient treatment. One advantage of the outpatient approach is that it usually enables workers to stay on the job, at least part-time.

Other sources of outpatient treatment include community mental health centers, which are partly financed by the government, and privately or publicly operated halfway houses, which offer free or inexpensive intermediate care consisting of food, shelter and support. . . .

Aversion therapy. Conditioning the alcoholic to abhor the taste, smell and sight of alcohol is the purpose of chemical aversion treatment, which usually requires special hospital facilities. Most such facilities are located in the West and Southwest. A substance called emetine is given just before an alcoholic drink. Nausea caused by the emetine follows, and if the treatment takes, the repeated association leaves the patient with a strong aversion to alcohol. Chemical aversion therapy appears to work best for alcoholics who are strongly motivated to control their disease. Dr. Saxe cautions in his report that, because nausea is repeatedly induced, the technique is potentially hazardous and must be administered under medical supervision. Aversion therapy is expensive, requiring about two weeks of hospitalization, with possible follow-up sessions. . . .

Which treatment when?

Any treatment is better than none. Total abstinence for a year is a popular yardstick for success, and that goal is reached on the average about 60% of the time.

That doesn't mean the alcoholic can enroll in any program and expect success. The alcoholic must want help. The discipline of the live-in setup may be right for some but not for others. Placing teenagers among chronic middle-age drinkers may be inappropriate. Matching patients to specific treatments or predicting favorable outcomes is a risky business; however, here are some guidelines to go by:

• The more affluent and the higher the social standing of the alcoholic, the better the chance of a sober outcome. Being employed and married, having the spouse involved in the treatment, accepting the diagnosis and drinking little or not at all during treatment are favorable signs of recovery, according to alcohol researcher Chad D. Emrick. Negative signs include previous inpatient treatment for alcoholism, aggressiveness, and one or more attempts at suicide.

• Generally speaking, alcoholics seem to respond better to group therapy and combinations of treatment than to a single approach. But the outcome is not influenced much by the length of the treatment or whether it is received on an inpatient or outpatient basis. Debatable, too, is the effectiveness of individual psychotherapy, particularly if the patient continues to drink during treatment.

• An estimated 10% of problem drinkers recover by themselves without treatment. But because nobody can predict who will, it would be a mistake for the alcoholic to forgo intervention.

Once you decide

More than 4,200 centers offer alcoholism treatment. Therapy in one form or another is available in every state, either in nonprofit clinics or in one of the growing number of units owned by for-profit health care chains, such as Comprehensive Care and National Medical Enterprises.

Competition for patients and scarce medical dollars is increasing the availability of treatment. That increase also boosts the odds of someone landing in an inappropriate treatment center, a good reason for the alcoholic or any would-be helper to proceed with caution when selecting treatment.

Be wary of extravagant promises that the battle of the bottle will be over at the end of treatment, says Richard Weedman of the National Association of Alcoholism Treatment Programs. Perhaps it will, but getting off alcohol is one thing, staying off is another. Programs that offer follow-up treatment and support have better records than those that let go of patients too soon.

Ask about the nature of the program and the type of patient treated. Professionals, for example, often do better in therapy groups of patients with interests similar to their own. Ask about the program's rate of success. Does success mean sobriety at the end of one year, for example, or longer? If there are doubts about the quality of the replies or the diagnosis, seek another opinion, says Dr. Robert Niven, director of the National Institute on Alcohol Abuse and Alcoholism.

Some 200 chapters of the National Council on Alcoholism can help steer alcoholics to reputable sources of treatment. Another clue to professionalism is recognition by the Joint Commission on Accreditation of Hospitals (JCAH), which has accredited more than 500 alcohol- and drug-abuse treatment centers. Accreditation indicates that the center has voluntarily opened its doors to outside scrutiny and complies with JCAH standards. By writing to the commission's marketing department (875 N. Michigan Ave., Chicago, Ill. 60611) with the name and address of any center you have in mind, you can learn whether it is accredited. Accreditation by the organization may facilitate insurance reimbursement. Insurance coverage for alcoholism varies, . . . so be sure appropriate benefits are included in your policy.

Be sure the facility under consideration is licensed by the state and, if the patient is elderly, is approved by medicare.

Informal and effective self-help is available from volunteer organizations, the most prominent being AA, which is supported by contributions from members only. Most sizable communities have a chapter listed in the phone book, and many communities have Al-Anon and Alateen for family members of alcoholics. The General Service Office of AA (P.O. Box 459, Grand Central Station, New York, N.Y. 10163) supplies information on request.

Source: *Changing Times*, August 1984, pp. 63–65.

rectly by family members or close friends who present evidence of the ways in which his or her drinking is destroying not only the problem drinker but the family unit as well.

Interventions should always be conducted under the supervision of a counselor trained in this field. Otherwise, they can easily disintegrate into shouting matches filled with threats and recriminations. The single aim of any intervention is to get the alcoholic into treatment. Usually, family members and close friends assemble with the alcoholic and read to him or her letters that have been written with the aid of the counselor. Specific examples of the alcoholic's behavior while under the influence are given, and, even more importantly, the devastating effect of this behavior on the family member in question is outlined. If necessary, everyone who participates in an intervention must be prepared to issue an ultimatum to the alcoholic and stick to it. Refusal to get help should have specific consequences to the alcoholic that family members are willing to enforce.

Statistics on the success rate of interventions are hard to come by, but professionals report that as many as 80 to 95 percent of alcoholics who are confronted in this way actually make it into some kind of treatment, whether inpatient or outpatient. [4] Of course, arrangements for treatment should be made *before* an intervention takes place. Once an alcoholic has agreed to seek help, no time should be lost in turning him or her over to professional care.

In cases where extreme physical dependence on alcohol has been established, the first step in any treatment process is **detoxification**. If the body's cells have adjusted to large quantities of alcohol, abrupt cessation of heavy drinking can precipitate extreme withdrawal symptoms, including seizures; **psychosis**; abrupt shifts in blood pressure, temperature, and pulse rate; and even death. For this reason, detoxification is best accomplished in a hospital-like

Detoxification: The process of removing all traces of a poisonous substance from the body; also used to describe the initial phase of alcoholism or substance abuse treatment.

Psychosis: A severe form of mental illness characterized by a deranged personality, delusions, or hallucinations.

Did You Know That . . .

Up to 50 percent of alcoholics relapse within 3 months of treatment.

setting, where **tranquilizers** can be administered and the alcoholic can receive adequate medical monitoring and supervision.

In cases of less advanced alcoholism, withdrawal is less dangerous and does not normally require medical intervention. Nonetheless, even "mild" withdrawal from alcohol after prolonged heavy drinking is likely to be quite unpleasant, accompanied by sweating, nervous tremors, rapid heart rate, and increased blood pressure.

Whether an alcoholic withdraws from alcohol with medical help or on his or her own, this process is only the very beginning of recovery. The biggest challenge for an alcoholic is not to stop drinking but to continue not to drink. Although many alcoholics move directly from detoxification programs to outpatient therapy and attendance at Alcoholics Anonymous meetings, inpatient rehabilitation is an increasingly popular alternative, especially for patients who have reached the advanced stages of alcoholism.

Inpatient rehabilitation can take place in hospital units or in freestanding facilities. During the 1970s and early 1980s, the number of these facilities proliferated, partly because they were increasingly seen as effective treatment settings and partly because more and more private insurance companies agreed to cover the costs. [5] Typically, inpatient treatment lasts anywhere from 4 weeks to 6 months, depending on the severity of the problem. Costs vary from facility to facility, but they are all steep; a 28-day stay can run anywhere from $5,000 to $10,000, and many facilities recommend treatment of longer duration. [6]

The biggest advantage of inpatient rehabilitation is that an alcoholic can begin his or her recovery in an environment free from the stresses of daily life. Inpatient rehabilitation can also provide support, encouragement, and reinforcement of an alcoholic's desire to stay sober. The alcoholic lives in an environment that prohibits the use of alcohol or any other nonprescription drug. Individual and group counseling, alcohol education, and the relearning of social skills are provided. Such a program offers an alcoholic a good head start on sobriety as he or she begins to learn how to cope with life without the crutch of alcohol.

After rehabilitation, many alcoholics are referred to **halfway houses**, supervised facilities that act as bridges between the hospital and the outside world. In most cases, halfway houses are recommended to those recovering alcoholics from extremely troubled homes and in cases where there is a minimal or nonexistent history of productive employment and family life. Halfway-house residents are usually required to hold down steady jobs—sometimes for the first time in their lives—but return to the halfway

Tranquilizers: Any of a variety of prescription drugs that depress the central nervous system, thus relieving anxiety and tension and sometimes relaxing the muscles.

Halfway houses: Residential treatment facilities for alcoholism and other disorders, where patients are allowed to participate in outside activities while in treatment.

FIGURE 5.3
Group Therapy

Many recovering alcoholics find regular group therapy sessions helpful in managing their anxieties and other emotions and in developing confidence in their new life-style.

house at night and during weekends. These facilities offer a setting in which the alcoholic develops solid personal relationships with nondrinkers, acquires social and coping skills, and learns about individual responsibility. The halfway-house experience can last from 3 months to 2 years.

An alternative to lengthy and expensive inpatient rehabilitation is intensive outpatient rehabilitation. Typically, this sort of treatment requires the patient to attend group counseling sessions 4 nights a week for 12 weeks. During these sessions, the newly recovering alcoholic learns how to deal with anxiety and conflict without recourse to alcohol. Usually, it is suggested that this be supplemented with attendance at AA meetings. Outpatient rehabilitation is available at a fraction of the cost of inpatient rehabilitation, and the less seriously impaired alcoholic can avail himself or herself of it without having to leave work, family, and community for a protracted period of time. During the

Did You Know That . . .

Alcoholics who have the most successful recoveries from their addiction have learned the importance of understanding themselves, have developed intimacy in their relationships, have improved coping skills, and have gained a sense of purpose in life.

late 1980s, insurance companies began to balk at the high cost of inpatient rehabilitation; [7] consequently, outpatient rehabilitation is an increasingly popular alternative.

Even after rehabilitation, whether inpatient or outpatient, is completed, the alcoholic is still considered to be in early recovery and is referred to some sort of aftercare program. Even after months of rehabilitation, the recovering alcoholic's sobriety is very fragile, and relapse, while by no means inevitable, is a constant danger. For this reason, some sort of ongoing counseling is indicated, and this further support can take several forms. Among these are individual therapy, group therapy, marital and family counseling, and self-help groups, including the most popular, Alcoholics Anonymous.

Regardless of which treatment mode is used, the goals are essentially the same: namely, to teach the recovering alcoholic that no matter how advanced his or her condition, it is possible to rebuild a full and productive life without slipping back into a reliance on alcohol to avoid life's problems. Therapy for alcoholics seeks to build self-esteem, to manage anxiety and other emotions such as anger, depression, frustration, guilt, and shame, and to hone the skills necessary to develop and maintain satisfying relationships.

ALCOHOLICS ANONYMOUS

Alcoholics Anonymous was founded in 1935 by a New York stockbroker and a surgeon from Ohio. Both were alcoholics who had nearly died from their malady. Bill Wilson and Bob Smith discovered that the cornerstone of their own continuing sobriety lay in helping their fellow sufferers to recover as they had done. According to figures provided by Alcoholics Anonymous, by 1989 the Fellowship had burgeoned into a worldwide organization with 1,793,834 members, 896,033 of them residents of the United States. [8]

Although statistics on rates of recovery are hard to come by, Alcoholics Anonymous is generally acknowledged as highly effective in the maintenance of long-term sobriety. Almost 30 percent of AA's members have 5 or more years of continuous sobriety; 38 percent have 1 to 5 years; and 33 percent are in their first year of recovery. [9]

AA is a true grass roots organization composed of thousands of local groups that meet in churches, schools, town halls, and other gathering places throughout the country. Although mem-

FIGURE 5.4
Alcoholics Anonymous

Alcoholics Anonymous is comprised of thousands of local groups that meet in churches, schools, town halls, and other gathering places throughout the country. Their primary purpose is to maintain the sobriety of each member and to help other suffering alcoholics achieve sobriety.

bers learn many of the practical life skills developed in formal therapy, AA is essentially a spiritual program that is based on the proposition that only by drawing on a power greater than the individual can the community sustain its common purpose, which is to maintain the sobriety of each member and to help other suffering alcoholics achieve sobriety.

(continued on p. 94)

Did You Know That . . .

Across the nation, about 32,000 AA groups and 4,500 rehabilitation clinics, hospitals, and outpatient facilities offer recovery programs.

Nan Robertson, author of . . . AA: Inside Alcoholics Anonymous, *is a journalist and reformed alcoholic. A* New York Times *reporter for more than 30 years, she won the Pulitzer Prize in 1983 for a personal account of her nearly fatal struggle with toxic-shock syndrome.*

"I'm One Drink Away From Being a Drunk"

Where would I be without Alcoholics Anonymous? I would be dead. I entered AA in 1975. I haven't had a drink in 12 years. But it took me years to get well, and I had a turbulent recovery, including hospitalization for a nervous breakdown. The most courageous act of my life was not to recover from toxic shock; it was to admit that I was a drunk and to do something about it.

The world is full of functioning alcoholics, and I was one of them. I didn't drink on the job for the longest time. I never lost my job through drinking. I didn't ruin my career. I would have done all of these things had I gone on for long enough.

For me, it was a conversation with one person who told me I had to stop, who was not himself an alcoholic but whose father had died an active alcoholic. It was the combination of this man's gentleness and his grief over his father and the fact that he was a doctor—but that really wasn't the important thing. It was that he had suffered through alcoholism. And somehow, what he had to say to me started me on the road back.

I began drinking alcoholically when I was 33, which was about the time I married my second husband, Stanley Levy. I was controlled for the 10 years of our marriage before his death by the fact that he was a moderate drinker, the fact that he loved me. I was careful about my drinking. After he died, very traumatically, all controls were off, and I began drinking suicidally, and did so from 1971, when Stan died, almost through 1975, when I went to Smithers (an intensive alcoholism-treatment center in New York City) and then immediately thereafter joined AA.

The worst-kept secret

I drank very heavily at night. My friends at work didn't know this. My editors didn't know this. I thought I'd kept the secret. But when I called up from Smithers joyfully telling everybody I'm an alcoholic, it was the worst-kept secret in the world. My mother had known, all my close friends had known and my stepson had known.

You know, alcoholics drink for every reason they can possibly find. Your life is structured around alcohol. I used to look forward to lunch all the time because there I could have a couple of martinis and a beer. That's pretty pathetic, isn't it? I always wanted to go to restaurants where drinks were served. I didn't want to go to coffee shops. It's very, very typical.

There's a dramatic difference between the way women alcoholics drink and the way men alcoholics drink, which has a lot to do with the way society views women who drink heavily. Women alcoholics generally are hidden alcoholics. It is much less socially acceptable for women to go to bars, to be drunk and disorderly publicly, so very often women drink at home. They often drink alone. Betty Ford is a classic case.

A debt of gratitude

People don't judge people in AA. People don't check up on you. They do not care what you did out there when you were drunk. All they care about is helping you now that you're trying to get sober. That's something that's very hard for outsiders to understand, how extremely flexible AA is. If I feel in crisis now, I'll go to meetings. I still go fairly regularly, but not as much as I did when I was in a terrible state. At most, I would go to AA meetings perhaps five times a week. Now, I go to about one a week, sometimes one every two weeks.

It's very hard, if your life has been saved by an organization—with your help, of course—not to feel deeply grateful to it.

If you are a member of a family that includes an alcoholic, don't protect him or her. Don't call the boss to say, "Fred is sick today and can't come to the office." Don't pour the liquor down the sink. Don't rant and rave. Don't threaten, unless you mean it, that "I'm leaving you."

You have to detach yourself from the person who is an alcoholic and find your own life, because the alcoholic wraps his arms around the bottle—and the family wraps its arms around the alcoholic, and all of their lives become distorted. Their lives are dedicated to the principle that they have to keep his secret and they have to protect their drunk and nobody must know.

What you can do is save your own life. One of the best ways to find help is in Al-Anon, for the families of alcoholics, to know that you're not alone. They teach you to have a life of your own.

The best question to ask yourself or ask about someone you love: Is drinking distorting any part of my life—my working life, my social life, my family life? If it is, then you've got problems. Also, if you are secretly worried about your drinking, chances are you have reason to be worried. All alcoholics are, in their own souls, worried about their drinking. They may deny it; it is a disease of denial. Some people would rather be crazy than be called a drunk. It's still something that people are ashamed of. There's a terrible stigma involved in saying: "I am a drunk. That's what I am. I'm a successful, charming, effective drunk that's sober, and I'm one drink away from a drunk."

—*Conversation with Beth Brophy*

Source: Nan Robertson, *U.S. News & World Report* (30 November 1987).

Did You Know That . . .

Alcoholic recovery rates can range from 50 percent to 85 percent, depending on how well a particular patient is matched to a specific program.

The principles of Alcoholics Anonymous were originally derived from the Oxford Movement, a religious movement that held public confession of wrongdoings and prompt atonement as the keys to salvation. Although the founders of AA recognized alcoholism as a physical and mental disorder that was beyond the control of the individual sufferer, they held that the malady of alcoholism was primarily a spiritual disorder. In fact, Bill Wilson speaks often of "character flaws" and "glaring personality defects" in his straightforward descriptions of active alcoholics and maintains that it is only through daily efforts to grow along spiritual lines that a problem drinker can get sober and stay sober.

In the book *Alcoholics Anonymous,* first published in 1939, the authors outlined "12 Suggested Steps of Recovery," which are still the foundation of the approach to recovery recommended by AA members. Basically, the steps urge recovering alcoholics to admit that their drinking has made their lives unmanageable and that they can achieve and maintain sobriety only through atoning for the negative consequences of their alcoholic behavior, by committing themselves to lead ethical lives, by carrying the AA message to others, and by relying on a power greater than their own unaided will in every aspect of their lives. [10]

To noninitiates, this may all sound suspiciously vague, even cult-like, but AA is *not* a religious organization, and each member is free to develop his or her own concept of a Higher Power. In fact, members overwhelmingly report that the sustaining power of their Fellowship lies in its enveloping spirit of down-to-earth warmth, regard, and understanding. Members are encouraged to attend meetings regularly, to get to know each other, to call each other on the phone in times of stress or loneliness, and to feel free to discuss their troubles honestly and openly. Over the course of months and years, regular attendance at AA meetings, a growing reliance on the **12 Steps** as a way of life, and the opportunity to help others as well as to be helped by them develop in active AA members the strength of character, resilience, and optimism that their dependence on alcohol denied them.

12 Steps: A generic label used to describe the 12 basic steps that serve as guidelines for the Alcoholics Anonymous treatment program, or similar guidelines used by other self-help groups.

FAMILIES OF ALCOHOLICS

During the 1970s and 1980s, increasing attention began to be paid to the ravages of alcoholism not just on the individual sufferer, but on his or her family as well. Founded by Bill Wilson's wife, Lois, Al-Anon was the first program developed to meet the

(continued on p. 96)

Many rehabilitation units urge patients to join Alcoholics Anonymous, whose 12 Steps have been used as a program of recovery from alcoholism. There are other self-help programs, dealing with problems other than alcohol, which adapt AA's 12 Steps, such as Narcotics Anonymous, Cocaine Anonymous, Drugs Anonymous, Overeaters Anonymous, etc.

12 Steps to a New Life

1. We admitted we were powerless over alcohol—that our lives had become unmanageable.
2. Came to believe that a Power greater than ourselves could restore us to sanity.
3. Made a decision to turn our will and our lives over to the care of God, *as we understood Him.*
4. Made a searching and fearless moral inventory of ourselves.
5. Admitted to God, to ourselves, and to another human being the exact nature of our wrongs.
6. Were entirely ready to have God remove all these defects of character.
7. Humbly asked Him to remove our shortcomings.
8. Made a list of all persons we had harmed, and became willing to make amends to them all.
9. Made direct amends to such people wherever possible, except when to do so would injure them or others.
10. Continued to take personal inventory and when we were wrong promptly admitted it.
11. Sought through prayer and meditation to improve our conscious contact with God, *as we understood Him,* praying only for knowledge of His will for us and the power to carry that out.
12. Having had a spiritual awakening as the result of these steps, we tried to carry this message to alcoholics and to practice these principles in all our affairs.

Source: The 12 Steps are reprinted and adapted with permission of Alcoholics Anonymous World Services, Inc. Permission to reprint and adapt the 12 Steps does not mean that AA has reviewed or approved the contents of this publication, nor that AA agrees with the views expressed herein. AA is a program of recovery from alcoholism—use of the 12 Steps in connection with programs and activities which are patterned after AA, but which address other problems, does not imply otherwise.

Did You Know That . . .

Excessive drinking is cited as a major factor in more than 50 percent of all divorces in the United States.

FIGURE 5.5
12 Step Programs

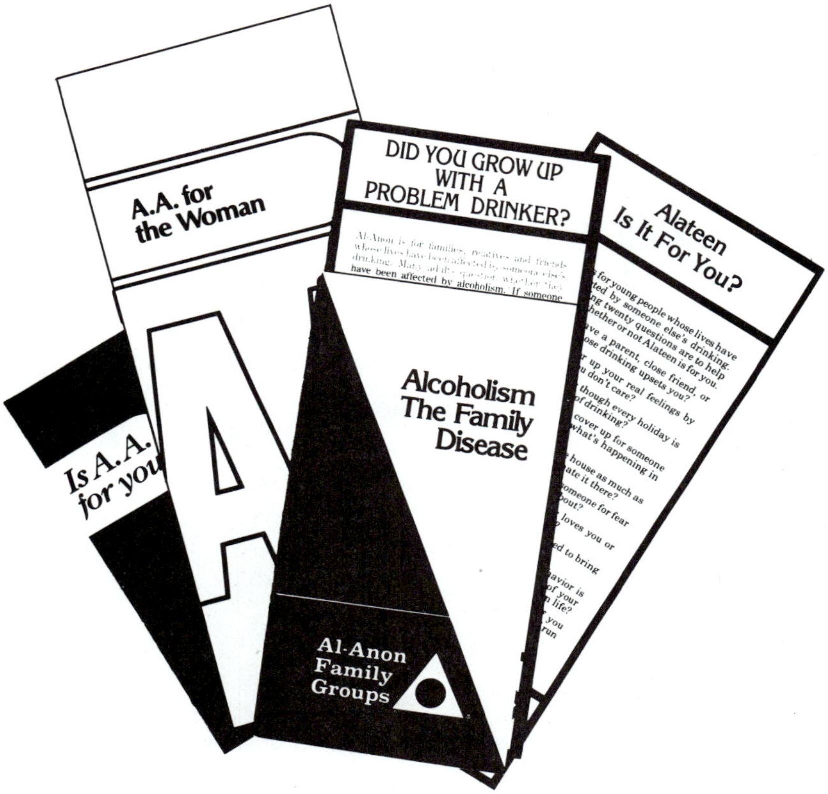

Besides treatment for the alcoholic, there are many organizations and groups that have formed to help the family and friends of the alcoholic: Al-Anon, Alateen, ACOA (Adult Children of Alcoholics). These are usually listed in the telephone directory.

needs of the families of alcoholics, and it is organized similarly to AA. Al-Anon encourages members to rely on each other for support and guidance and suggests that the 12 Steps are the best tools for living a sane and useful life even if one's spouse or child continues in the active stages of alcoholism. Participants learn how to live with an active alcoholic without exacerbating the problem and how to extricate their lives from the alcoholic's, with all its attendant volatility and unpredictability.

Table 5.1
Has Drinking Ever Been a Cause of Trouble in Your Family?

	Yes: (in percentages)
1987	24
1985	21
1984	17
1981	22
1978	22
1976	17
1974	12
1966	12
1950	14

Source: *Index to International Public Opinion,* Vol. 1950, p. 459.

Alcoholism among family members is responsible for a large percentage of divorces, child abuse, and other family problems.

Children of alcoholics are almost invariably damaged in varying degrees by having to grow up in a household influenced by alcoholism. Often, marital discord is the rule in such situations, with children inevitably caught in the crossfire of their parents' sometimes violent quarrels. However erroneously, such children frequently conclude that they are responsible for the disharmony in their homes and suffer attendant guilt, anxiety, and low self-esteem. Tragically, neglect and child abuse, both physical and sexual, are often the rule in families headed by an alcoholic parent.

Adult children of alcoholics often report that despite the chaos of their homes, one or both parents expected them to act as if the situation were entirely normal, especially in their dealings with the outside world. Maintaining such fiction takes a terrible toll on children and tends to turn them into loners who shun normal relationships with their peers. Shame, mistrust, and a fear of intimacy are often constants in the lives of these children.

Of course, it is difficult to predict how children growing up in alcoholic households will turn out. However, there are some general tendencies. Many children of alcoholics experience the world as unsafe, have an inordinate fear of rejection, lack basic trust, avoid intimacy, have trouble with interpersonal relationships, are overly impulsive, and are incapable of tolerating frustration. [11]

(continued on p. 100)

Children of Alcoholics

Sometimes it's like running in quicksand. Sometimes it's like trying to find your way when you're blindfolded. Sometimes it's peaceful and then suddenly it may be chaos, and you never know what to expect. You live in fear of the unknown, and ask yourself: "Can I bring friends home today?"

Being the child of an alcoholic is like that. Not all the time, of course. There are good times, when your mom and dad are sober and things seem as normal as they are at your best friend's house. You love your parents, no question about that, but sometimes you are *so* angry with them.

Experts say it's natural to have these confused feelings, because life with an alcoholic parent is inconsistent and confusing. It's a little less confusing if you understand how life with an alcoholic parent affects you. Or, if you have a friend with an alcoholic parent, it helps to know what he or she is going through. You may have a friend like that, even though you don't know it. There are 28 million children in the United States with at least one alcoholic parent. Put another way, in your class of 25 students, four to six may be children of alcoholics.

Many of them don't realize how life in an alcoholic family shapes their attitudes and personality. For one thing, children of alcoholics have a hard time figuring out what's real and what isn't, because in an alcoholic family, reality is denied. One night there may be drinking and fighting and abuse. The next morning, parents act as if nothing happened. Children learn not to trust their parents, but they also learn not to trust their own instincts and feelings. In fact, Claudia Black, one of the first psychologists to write about children of alcoholics (called COAs), says these children are taught three sacred family rules: Don't talk, don't trust, don't feel.

ROLE-PLAYING

They learn some other lessons, too, according to Sharon Wegscheider-Cruse, another pioneer in working with children of alcoholics. They learn to play a role within their family that helps them get along at the moment, to keep things as stable as they can. But this may be harmful in the long run. Children of alcoholics take on one of these four roles:

- *Hero.* This usually is the oldest child. He or she is a superachiever who brings success to the family. Later in life, the hero may be a workaholic, unable to relax and have fun. And there's usually a sense of failure, because no matter how successful the hero is at school or work, he or she is not able to make the parent stop drinking.
- *Scapegoat.* This child takes the blame for the family problems. He or she may fail in school, take drugs, or get in trouble with the law. The scapegoat diverts negative attention from the real family problems by letting the world think he or she—rather than the alcoholic parent—is the problem. As they grow up, scapegoats may continue to be troublemakers.
- *Lost child.* This may be the middle child, who is quiet and never gives anyone any trouble. This is the child who never acts out in the classroom, so the teacher may overlook him or her. As adults, these persons may be afraid to let their needs be known, and they often fear any anger or conflict.
- *Mascot.* This is often the youngest child, who is doted on by all family members. This child's job is to be cute and entertaining and divert the family's attention when things are about to explode. In school, this is often the class clown. As an adult, the mascot may continue to avoid responsibility, thinking it's enough to be charming.

"DON'T FEEL"

All these children have one thing in common: They deny their feelings about family problems so thoroughly that they stop being able to understand their feelings about anything.

And since their relationships are often based

on a phony self, they never learn how to build close ties to another person. Claudia Black says that when COAs reach young adulthood, they may "begin to experience loneliness that doesn't make sense to them. They become aware of feelings that separate them from others, and they find themselves depressed."

Until the '70s, no one knew very much about the special problems of children of alcoholics. Now, however, COAs can read several books on the subject or join a group with other children of alcoholics to understand themselves better. For young children still at home, there are groups at school and at community mental health centers. Alateen is a wonderful resource, patterned after Alcoholics Anonymous (for alcoholics) and Al-Anon (for family and friends).

In these groups, children learn protective skills: that they have the right to refuse to drive with a parent who has been drinking, and that it's safest to stay out of the way when a parent is drunk.

They learn that their parent's drinking problem is not their fault. They did not cause the drinking and there is nothing they can do to stop it. They can, however, learn to get on with their life and not let the parent's drinking become the center of their whole existence.

And they can learn the facts of their own vulnerability to alcoholism. Children of alcoholics are four times as likely as other children to become alcoholics, and even more likely to marry one. Knowing this can make them more careful about their behavior.

Being the child of an alcoholic is not easy, but it's no longer a dark and scary mystery. Armed with the facts and supported by people who understand, COAs can look forward to a life of pride, achievement, and loving relationships.

PARENTS CAN BE CHILDREN OF ALCOHOLICS, TOO

If your parent drinks too much, remember that he or she may have grown up as a child of an alcoholic. Here are some things we know about adult children of alcoholics:

- They are afraid of intimate relationships. It's hard for them to trust others and it takes a lot of effort for them to get close to anyone, even their own children.
- They are afraid of authority. That makes it hard for them to act "parental" and set realistic limits for their children. Limits help children feel secure.
- Because they could not control their parents' drinking, they try to control other things. They may try to control their children's behavior, smothering them with overprotectiveness and not allowing them freedom.
- They want to give their children a better life than they had, but they may become jealous of their children for having that better life.

STRAIGHT TALK FOR CHILDREN OF ALCOHOLICS

1. You are not alone.
2. Your parents' alcoholism is not your fault.
3. You can get help for yourself. Here are a few suggestions:

Children of Alcoholics Foundation, Inc.
555 Madison Avenue
4th Floor
New York, NY 10022
(212) 754-0656

National Association for Children of Alcoholics
31582 Coast Highway
Suite B
South Laguna, CA 92677
(714) 499-3889

Al-Anon/Alateen Family Group Headquarters, Inc.
P.O. Box 182, Madison Square Station
New York, NY 10159-0182

For information about alcoholism-related services in your area, look in the Yellow Pages under "Alcoholism," or call your local department of public health for guidance.

—Sandra R. Arbetter, M.S.W.

Source: Sandra R. Arbetter, *Current Health* (February 1990), pp. 14–16.

Did You Know That . . .

More than 50 percent of juvenile delinquents come from alcoholic families. Many children of alcoholics have learning disabilities, and many other children of alcoholics may become overachievers to compensate for troubles at home.

Variables that seem to influence the impact of alcoholism on children include the number of brothers and sisters in the family, their ages, and the child's place in the birth order; when and how long the alcoholic was active, in treatment, and in recovery; and the availability of the nonalcoholic spouse, members of the extended family, and other supportive people, such as personal friends, friends of the family, teachers, and clergy. Finally, the effect of alcoholism on a growing child will be affected by that child's own inner resources and resilience, or lack thereof.

Like alcoholics themselves, many adult children of alcoholics find it very difficult to recognize and acknowledge the extent to which their lives have been warped by alcohol. Trained in childhood to keep the reality of their home lives secret, they carry this tendency into adulthood. Also, between one-fourth and one-third of the children of alcoholics become alcoholics themselves. [12] Adult children of alcoholics are also at risk for involvement with and even marriage to alcoholics.

It is understandable that children of alcoholics would wish to avoid the painful memories of their pasts. However, it is only by facing and working through the pain and conflict of their childhoods that they can come to terms with the distress that undermines them and go on to live full and happy lives.

During the 1980s, the 12 Step program offered by Adult Children of Alcoholics (ACOA) became an increasingly popular resource for individuals victimized by the alcoholism of one or both parents. Like Alcoholics Anonymous, this self-help group gives members the opportunity to share painful memories and experiences with a community that understands and supports them. Participants report that such fellowship alleviates the shame and guilt that are the legacies of their youth and allows them to put the past behind them and get on with their lives. Participation in ACOA is often an adjunct to professional counseling, where each patient's unique issues can be addressed and resolved.

TREATING THE FAMILY

Family therapy applies therapeutic techniques to its members in the interest of effecting constructive changes in their thinking and behavior. Family therapy for alcoholism is based on the assumption that it is not just the alcoholic but his or her entire family that needs help because members have gradually adopted a whole range of dysfunctional behaviors in order to cope with a chaotic, unpredictable, and frequently violent environment. However unhealthy these coping patterns may be, they seem to work and become a "steady state" or equilibrium that allows individual members to continue to function. Family therapy brings the members of a family together to face and, ideally, overcome the pathologies that govern their interactions.

HOW EFFECTIVE IS TREATMENT?

There is no overestimating the tenacity of addiction. No matter how destructive the consequences of alcohol and drug abuse, victims often persist in it literally to the death. Despite the wide range of treatment options that became available during the 1970s and 1980s, the rates of addiction and relapse after treatment have not fallen appreciably during that time.

This is not to say that the situation is hopeless. However, regardless of which road to recovery any given alcoholic chooses, his or her success ultimately rests on the commitment and determination he or she brings to the task of getting and staying well. Education, **behavior modification** techniques, and long-term rehabilitation can help enormously, but, finally, the recovering alcoholic, with whatever outside assistance, must somehow summon the inner strength to resist for a lifetime the temptation to drink again. Perhaps this is why Alcoholics Anonymous, of all the approaches tried, is the most successful–because its members acknowledge that for the rest of their lives the price of their continued sobriety is a daily renewal of their passionate desire to maintain it.

Behavior modification: A type of therapy based upon the system of reward and punishment for specific actions.

CHAPTER

6 Getting It Under Control

MOST AMERICANS WHO DRINK do so responsibly and in moderation. As we have seen, however, those who abuse alcohol not only do grievous damage to themselves and their loved ones, they also place an onerous burden on society at large, straining the health-care system, causing lowered productivity and morale on the job, endangering public safety, and creating carnage on the nation's highways.

As we saw in chapter 5, there are more treatment options available today to the suffering alcoholic than at any other time in history. But what is society doing to protect itself from the damage done by those alcoholics who do *not* seek treatment or, having sought it, fall back into their old drinking habits and behaviors? Increasingly, on the state level, individuals and communities are seeking redress through the courts, fighting for and enacting a series of laws that calls for stiff penalties for alcohol-impaired driving; punishment for those who hold the public safety in their hands, such as train engineers and airplane pilots, who drink on the job; and regulations that seek to hold those who serve alcohol, both in drinking establishments and in their own homes, accountable for the harm those they serve may do while under the influence.

DRINKING AND DRIVING

Among the first remedies sought to cut the rate of alcohol-impaired driving crashes was to raise the drinking age to 21. By the mid-1970s, while many 18- to 21-year-olds were serving in the armed forces during the Vietnam War, many states lowered the

Recognizing the Problem

Drinking is common in business. But when does it become alcoholism? To begin with, social drinkers do not require alcohol every day just to function (or have difficulty in situations where alcohol is not available), nor do they significantly increase their intake over the years. Being intoxicated for more than a few hours, and certainly for days at a time, is a clear sign of alcoholism. So is losing memory of what has happened in the past couple of hours or days.

Alcoholics always have substantial impairment of normal family, social, and occupational relationships. Socially, alcoholics tend to say or do things that embarrass others around them. On the job they may smell of alcohol, announce that they have a hangover or withdraw to nurse one, or have unexplained absences from work. Monday absenteeism (to recover from a bender) is as telling in an executive as in a production-line worker. Furtive trips to the file cabinet or sneaking away from work at odd times to take a drink can be other signs but may be hard to recognize if an executive keeps his or her own files or calendar.

Source: *Harvard Medical School Health Letter*, 3 September 1990, p. 4.

legal drinking age to 18. The reasoning, of course, was that if someone was old enough to die for his or her country on foreign soil, he or she was old enough to buy a drink. However, once the drinking age had been lowered, injuries and deaths involving young drivers doubled and tripled: by 54 percent in Michigan, for example, and by 100 percent in Massachusetts. The most significant increase came from nighttime collisions involving 18- to 21-year-old males, almost all of which were alcohol-related.

Alarmed and hoping to reverse the escalating trend, many state legislators began to call for a federally mandated legal drinking age of 21. Federal legislation was preferable because only then could the practice of buying alcohol in a state where it could be purchased legally at age 18 and transporting it across state lines be discouraged. In 1984, the Reagan administration passed the "21" law, which penalized states with a drinking age under 21 by withholding 5 percent of their federal highway funds. By the middle of 1987, 37 states had raised the drinking age to 21. By 1990, all states had enacted the 21-year-old drinking age law.

Raising the drinking age has saved lives. In 1975, 8,996 drivers aged 18 to 20 died. In 1984, 7,797 died–1,199 fewer

Did You Know That . . .

Although the number of drunk-driving fatalities in the United States has declined since 1982 due to more strict law enforcement, an estimated 40 percent of all Americans will still be involved in one alcohol-related accident during their lives.

FIGURE 6.1

Minimum Drinking Age and Estimated Lives Saved

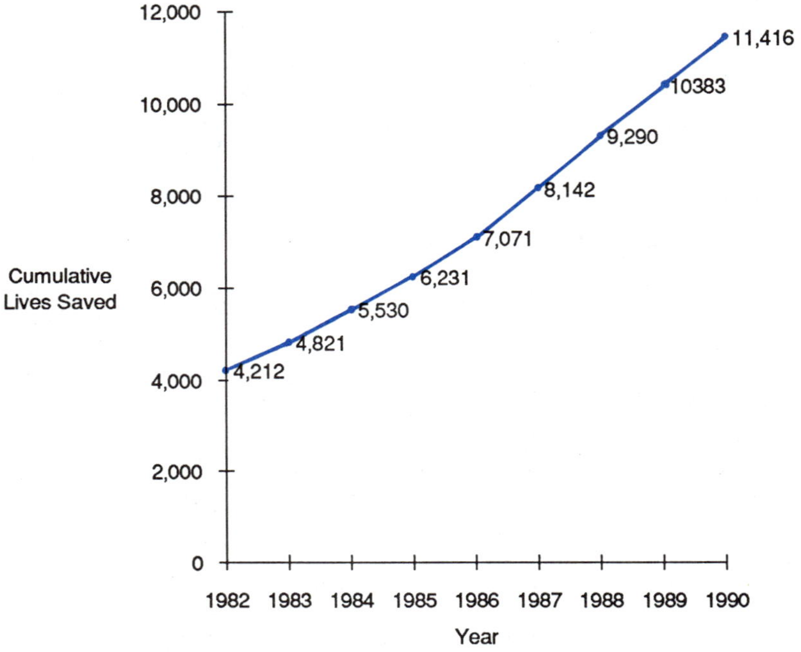

Source: Department of Transportation, National Highway Traffic Safety Administration.

It is estimated that Minimum Drinking Age (MDA) laws have saved over 11,400 lives since 1975. This graph depicts in visual form the cumulative lives saved by MDAs over the 9-year period from 1982 through 1990.

deaths. [1] At least 30 percent of this reduction in fatalities has been attributed to raising the drinking age.

With increased knowledge of the effects of alcohol on the nervous system and the development of sophisticated devices for measuring blood alcohol level, legislators have also taken steps to establish a legal definition of intoxication, based on blood alcohol content (BAC). By the early 1960s, scientists were able to designate a blood alcohol level of 0.10 percent as the limit beyond which most fatal accidents occurred. In 1966, a federal standard of 0.10 percent BAC for intoxication was established, and states were urged to adopt it. By 1990, only Georgia's BAC level, at 0.12

FIGURE 6.2
Testing for Blood Alcohol Levels

The breathalyzer makes it possible for law enforcement officers to determine a suspect's blood alcohol concentration by measuring the amount of alcohol exhaled in a breath.

percent, exceeded this recommendation; several states, including California, Maine, Oregon, Utah, and Vermont, established a 0.08 percent BAC limit. In 1985, the American Medical Association (AMA) urged all states to set the legal limit much lower—at 0.05 percent BAC. In 1988, the Surgeon General of the United States urged the states to follow the AMA's recommendation or to apply the BAC currently applied to commercial transportation workers, which at that time was 0.04 percent. The Surgeon General also recommended that the permissible BAC for drivers under the age of 21 should be established at 0.00 percent nationally. Today, any driver with a BAC of 0.10 or higher can be arrested for **Driving While Intoxicated (DWI)**. Nearly every state has set up weekend roadblocks, called "sobriety checkpoints" to help enforce the law.

During the 1980s, numerous laws aimed at bars, clubs, and restaurants were enacted. Most laws prohibit bars from serving obviously intoxicated customers. There are "killer bar" statutes that allow judges to ask defendants where they had their last drink. Then they issue warnings to and exact stiff fines from those bars that do not refuse service to inebriated customers. Some states prohibit bars from holding evening "happy hours," when drinks are served at discount prices. "Happy hour" laws may prohibit serving one person more than 2 drinks at a time. Lawsuits for millions of dollars have been filed and won against bars serving drunk customers who have subsequently caused fatal accidents. As a result of legal suits, liquor liability insurance costs have skyrocketed, putting some bars and even some insurance companies out of business.

A few states, including New Jersey and Indiana, have enacted "social host liability laws," under which a host or hostess in a private home can be sued if someone leaves the party intoxicated and causes an accident. People who entertain with alcohol are urged to serve it in moderation and to insist that an inebriated guest either get a ride with a sober driver, take a taxi home, or spend the night.

Just as laws vary from state to state, penalties for alcohol-impaired driving also vary. Predictably, as the legislative assault on alcohol-impaired driving escalates, so does the severity of penalties imposed for this crime. In general, penalties are assessed on the basis of whether or not the alcohol-impaired driver is a first-time offender. In general, first-time offenders face suspension of their licenses from 30 to 90 days, monetary fines, and mandated community service. Second- and third-time offenders often face suspension of their licenses for up to 2 years, mandatory attendance at alcohol education seminars or Alcoholics Anonymous meetings, and sometimes even jail time. A vehicular homicide caused by DWI is designated as a **felony** in most states. A typical penalty would be a mandatory minimum 6-month jail sentence, suspension of license, alcohol education, and stiff fines.

Grass roots outrage over drunk driving has been responsible for enacting much of the new legislation against it. Perhaps the most influential organization in this campaign has been **Mothers Against Drunk Driving (MADD)**, founded in 1980 by Candy

(continued on p. 108)

Driving While Intoxicated (DWI): Operating a motor vehicle while under the influence of alcohol or other intoxicating drug.

Felony: A major criminal offense, especially one punishable by substantial fine or imprisonment.

Mothers Against Drunk Driving (MADD): A voluntary group founded in 1980 that provides support to victims of drunk drivers and their families and lobbies for tougher policies to curb drunk driving.

Candy Lightner's Crusade

The problem: how to cut down on drunk driving, which was killing about 28,000 Americans every year.

Candy Lightner had a horrible reason for wanting to achieve that goal. On May 3, 1980, her 13-year-old daughter Cari was walking to a church carnival in Fair Oaks, Calif., when a car swerved out of control and killed her. Police arrested a 46-year-old cannery worker named Clarence Busch and found that he had a long record of arrests for intoxication. Less than a week earlier, he had been bailed out on a hit-and-run drunk-driving charge. A policeman told Lightner that Busch was unlikely to spend any time behind bars for killing her daughter: drunk driving was just one of those things.

Lightner, then 33, a divorced real estate agent with two other children, heard that judgment as she was on her way to a dinner with friends on the eve of her daughter's funeral. She was still furious when she joined them in a cocktail lounge as they waited for a table. It was there, of all places, that she decided to do something. "I remember sitting in the bar with all these people and saying out loud, 'I'm going to start an organization.' Just like that. There was this big moment of silence, and then my girlfriend pipes up and says, 'And we can call it Mothers Against Drunk Drivers.' I didn't have a plan, a goal, nothing. All I knew was that I was going to start an organization, and I was determined to make it work."

She went to see California Governor Jerry Brown to persuade him to appoint a task force to deal with drunk driving. Brown declined to receive her. She went to his office every day, talking to anyone who would listen. After newspapers publicized Lightner's crusade, Brown finally told her that he was appointing the task force and that she would be a member. "I just started crying right there in his office," Lightner says.

Once launched, Mothers Against Drunk Driving (MADD) proved a virtually irresistible force. Now headquartered near Dallas, where Lightner moved, MADD has 320 chapters nationwide and 600,000 volunteers and donors. In response to Lightner's efforts, California passed a tough new law in 1981 that imposes minimum fines of $375 and mandatory imprisonment of up to four years for repeat offenders. By now all 50 states have tightened their drunk-driving laws. And Lightner keeps making speeches, lobbying legislators and generally creating waves. [In] July [1984] she stood beside President Ronald Reagan as he signed a new law reducing federal highway grants to any state that fails to raise the drinking age to 21. Her next goals: an indemnity fund for victims, a bill of rights for victims, automatic imprisonment for repeat offenders. (Clarence Busch did finally serve 21 months in jail for the death of Cari Lightner.)

FIGURE 6.3

Mothers Against Drunk Driving

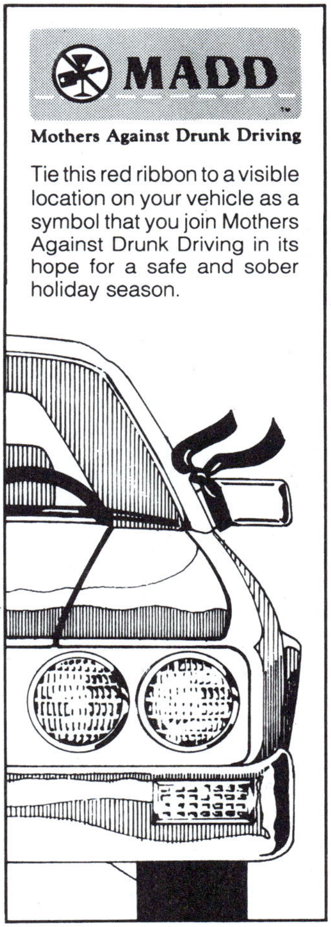

The mission of Mothers Against Drunk Driving is to stop drunk driving and provide support to victims and their families.

"I believe that for every problem there is a solution," Lightner says. "We are changing the way people think about drinking and driving. But more than that, we have caused people to change their behavior, and that is saving lives. I believe in the rights of victims. And I do feel that if you believe in something badly enough, you can make a difference."

Source: Candy Lightner, "You Can Make a Difference," *Time* (7 January 1985), p. 41.

Lightner, a California woman whose 13-year-old daughter was killed by a hit-and-run alcohol-impaired driver. MADD is a nationwide nonprofit corporation with half a million supporters and members. There are chapters of MADD in Canada, Great Britain, and New Zealand. According to MADD's central office in Fort Worth, Texas, 400 new alcohol-impaired driving laws have been passed in the United States since 1981. As a result of MADD's efforts, media attention, and other citizen-group action, juries are now more sympathetic to the rights of the victim than they are to the rights of the alcohol-impaired driver. MADD believes that strict criminal prosecution of alcohol-impaired drivers is the most effective deterrent in reducing the menace of alcohol-impaired driving.

Young people themselves are also taking action against alcohol-impaired driving. In many high schools and colleges throughout the country, students have established chapters of **Students Against Driving Drunk (SADD)**, an organization that was initiated in the early 1980s by Robert Anastos, a teacher from Massachusetts. SADD's approach, and that of similar peer-centered programs, is primarily educational; that is, to make young people aware of the dangers of driving after drinking even small amounts of alcohol. According to a June 14, 1990, article in the *Wall Street Journal,* SADD received 400,000 requests for its parent-student contracts, in which teens agree not to drink and drive, between January and June of 1990. There are SADD chapters in about 80 percent of U.S. high schools.

Although most efforts on the part of teenagers to combat alcohol-impaired driving recognize that it is preferable for young people not to drink at all, most of them also accept the fact that many teenagers *do* drink despite the fact that it is illegal and potentially harmful to them emotionally and physically. Recognizing this, organizations such as Safe Rides have been set up to provide transportation home for inebriated teens with no questions asked. The reasoning, obviously, is that if a teenager has had too much to drink, the most important goal is to discourage

Students Against Driving Drunk (SADD): A student group founded in the early 1980s to educate young people about the dangers of driving drunk.

FIGURE 6.4
Parent-Teenager Contract

CONTRACT FOR LIFE

A Contract for Life Between Parent and Teenager

Under this contract, we understand S.A.D.D. encourages all youth to adopt a no use policy and obey the laws of their state with regards to alcohol and illicit drugs.

Teenager I agree to call you for advice and/or transportation at any hour from any place if I am ever faced with a situation where a driver has been drinking or using illicit drugs. I have discussed with you and fully understand your attitude toward any involvement with underage drinking or the use of illegal drugs.

____
Signature

Parent I agree to come and get you at any hour, any place, no questions asked and no argument at that time, or I will pay for a taxi to bring you home safely. I expect we would discuss this at a later time.

I agree to seek safe, sober transportation home if I am ever in a situation where I have had too much to drink or a friend who is driving me has had too much to drink.

____
Signature

____
Date

STUDENTS AGAINST DRIVING DRUNK S A D D ®

Distributed by S.A.D.D., "Students Against Driving Drunk"

Source: Students Against Driving Drunk.

The SADD drinking-driver contract provides an opportunity for family discussion of a serious problem. By signing it, both teenager and parent acknowledge their responsibilities to one another.

Did You Know That . . .

In one survey of 2,200 private and professional pilots, 16 percent of the respondents admitted to drinking more than 5 drinks per occasion 2 or more times a month, or more than 2 drinks per day, which is about the same rate as that of the general population.

him or her from getting behind the wheel of a car, and to worry about any possible drinking problem later. This is especially true since, as we noted in chapter 3, alcohol-impaired driving is the leading cause of death among youths between the ages of 15 and 24.

COMMERCIAL TRANSPORTATION

In a speech in New York City in September 1986, James Burnett, chairman of the National Transportation Safety Board, reported, "One-half of all rapid-transit accidents we investigated in the last couple of years have been due to drugs, legal and illicit, and/or alcohol. We can't prove direct causal effect, but the problem was certainly there."

The Federal Railroad Administration reported that alcohol and drug use played a part in approximately 48 accidents causing 37 deaths, 80 injuries, and $34.4 million in damages between 1975 and 1984. As a routine measure, the Federal Railroad Administration now tests new employees for drug use and also tests current employees whom supervisors suspect of alcohol and other drug use.

Partly in response to these alarming statistics and in reaction to growing concern about alcohol abuse among the public, Congress passed a law in 1986 that prohibits alcohol and other drug use by commercial transport employees. Under this law, the maximum penalty for those convicted is 15 years in jail and a $250,000 fine. On August 20, 1990, a federal jury delivered the first conviction under this law, finding 3 pilots for Northwest Airlines guilty of flying a jetliner under the influence of alcohol. The 3 pilots were arrested after they flew from North Dakota to Minneapolis. A bar patron had notified federal officials that he had seen the three drinking heavily the night before in a bar. In blood tests taken 2 hours after the plane had landed safely, one pilot had a 0.13 percent BAC, far in excess of the legal limit of 0.04 percent the Federal Aviation Administration sets for pilots. The copilot and the flight engineer had BACs of 0.06 percent and 0.08 percent, respectively.

Even before the verdict, the case of the 3 pilots had become the heart of a new campaign for tougher federal standards on drinking and flying. The 1986 law prohibits anyone under the influence of alcohol or drugs from transporting commercial passengers across state lines. But unlike state alcohol-impaired driving laws, it does not specify a permissible level of alcohol in the driver's or pilot's blood. That left the prosecution in the Northwest Airlines case with the task of convincing the jury that the 3 Northwest pilots were under the influence of alcohol. Federal guidelines call for a sentence of 12 to 18 months in prison for first offenders in cases of this kind.

"The message the jury has sent is that the public is deeply concerned and fearful of pilots who fly while under the influence of alcohol," said James L. Oberstar, the Minnesota democrat who chairs the Aviation Subcommittee of the House Public Works and Transportation Committee.

In responding to news of the verdict, Jay Winsten, director of the alcohol project at the Harvard School of Public Health, said the verdict reflected the nation's growing intolerance with drinking in situations that can endanger others. People view such offenses as "equivalent to playing Russian roulette," he said, adding, "You don't have to wait for that live chamber to go off for a crime to be committed." [2]

CHANGING ATTITUDES

Although Americans are taking an increasingly punitive stand against alcohol abuse as it affects public safety on the highways and in the workplace, there is also a growing acceptance of the fact that alcoholics are sick people who need help. This, of course, is reflected in the enormous growth of alcoholism treatment facilities throughout the country.

There has also been an increased emphasis on prevention; that is, on recognizing early signs of alcohol abuse and urging the person in question to seek help before the problem gets completely out of hand. In industry and in schools, such efforts have taken the form of **employee assistance programs (EAPs)** and **student assistance programs (SAPs)**, respectively.

In both EAPs and SAPs, supervisors and teachers are alert to deteriorating performance and behavior changes. If there is reason to believe that these danger signs are alcohol-related, an evaluation by a professional alcoholism counselor is recommended. Many problem drinkers have found their way into treatment before advanced alcoholism has been established by these sorts of early interventions. In most cases, the employee or student in question is welcomed back to his or her job or classroom after recovery has begun.

For the most part, efforts to prevent alcohol abuse are aimed at those young people who are felt to be at "high risk," including

Employee assistance programs (EAP): Counseling programs provided as a fringe benefit to employees by their employers; such programs come in a variety of forms and offer services ranging from substance abuse counseling to long-term therapy.

Student assistance programs (SAP): Counseling programs provided by schools and other educational institutions to their students; as with employee assistance programs, the services offered vary from program to program.

FIGURE 6.5
Estimated U.S. per Capita Consumption of Pure Alcohol, 1977–1987

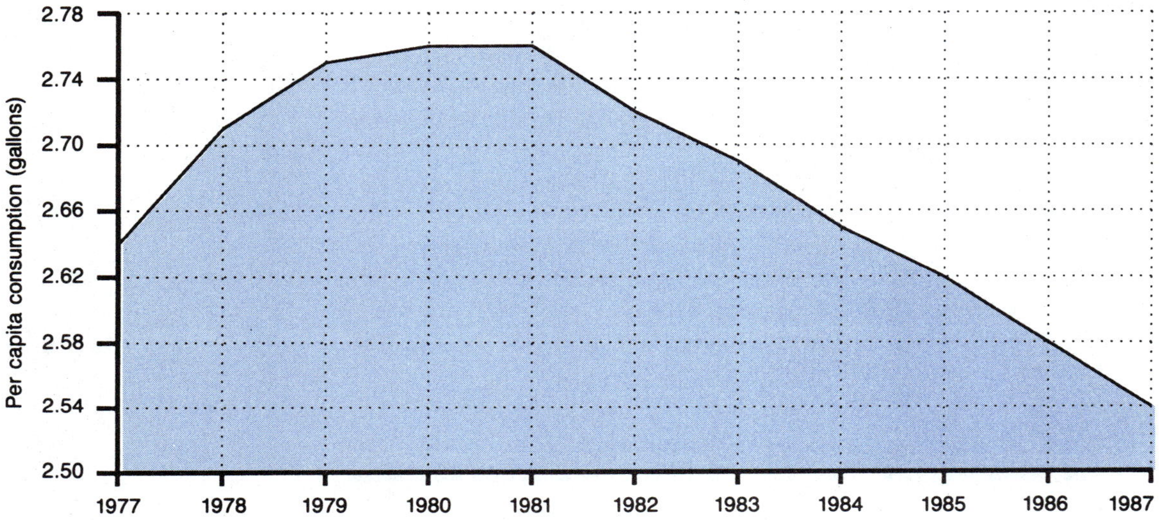

Source: National Institute on Alcohol Abuse and Alcoholism, 1989.

The best available estimates suggest that per capita alcohol consumption has decreased steadily since 1981. This decrease may be related to increased public awareness of the risks of alcohol use and an increasing concern with health and fitness.

Gateway drugs: A label applied to legal (licit) drugs such as alcohol, nicotine, and caffeine that are thought to serve as "gateways" to the use of other intoxicating substances, especially the so-called hard drugs.

Latchkey children: Term used to describe young children who are left alone for all or a substantial portion of the day, especially children whose parent or parents work outside the home.

abused and neglected children, the homeless or runaways, **gateway drug** (alcohol, marijuana, and nicotine) users, the physically or mentally handicapped, pregnant teens, school dropouts, children of alcohol and other drug abusers, **latchkey children**, and the poor. [3] Authorized by Congress in the Anti-Drug Abuse Act of 1986, the Office of Substance Abuse Prevention (OSAP) provides support nationwide to public and nonprofit private organizations to develop various approaches to prevent alcohol and other drug abuse among these high-risk populations. These model programs involve schools, local agencies, juvenile justice and probationary systems, parent groups, and others who are concerned with young people.

Prevention on this level primarily involves helping those at risk for alcohol and other drug abuse find solutions to their problems, thus mitigating the helplessness and despair that can lead to this abuse. For example, efforts might be made to help unemployed teens enter the job market or to encourage high school dropouts to become reinvolved in an educational or vocational training program. Young people with emotional problems are encouraged to seek some sort of counseling rather than relying on alcohol to ease the pain. After-school programs are developed to take care of children who would otherwise come home to empty houses every day.

The National Institute on Alcohol Abuse and Alcoholism (NIAAA) helps to develop educational programs that stress the harm alcohol abuse can do to the individual, that promote anti-drug abuse attitudes, and that encourage the adoption of appropriate behavioral skills to resist social pressures to drink and use drugs. NIAAA also supports research into such issues as pricing and availability, since studies have suggested that increases in pricing or decreases in availability of alcohol lower not only consumption but also the incidence of alcohol-related medical disorders and traumatic injuries.

HOPEFUL SIGNS AMONG THE YOUNG

In February 1988, James C. Callahan, a young student at Rutgers University in New Jersey, died from alcohol poisoning several hours after consuming massive quantities of alcohol as part of a fraternity initiation ceremony. The tragic death focused the nation's attention on the problems of alcohol abuse among not only fraternity members, but among college and university students in general. The initial response among college administrators to the incident at Rutgers was one of sharp concern, but they also voiced the conviction that there was little to be done about the widespread use of alcohol on their campuses. As one Yale administrator put it, "What it comes back to is you can do a lot with education, but individual people are still responsible if they choose to drink excessively. It's foolish to think you can stop that." [4]

Happily, in the years since Callahan's death, there are signs that the many alcohol education programs and policies in place on the nation's campuses are beginning to make a difference. Fraternities themselves have taken some steps to cope with alcohol abuse among their members. For example, a few years ago several fraternities formed the Fraternity Insurance Purchasing Group in an effort to keep liability insurance affordable. They developed guidelines concerning alcohol use among the group's members. Some of their policies include banning the bulk purchase of beer by fraternity houses, banning open keg parties

Did You Know That . . .

In 1980 93.2 percent of private and public high school seniors admitted to having used alcohol, compared to 90.7 percent in 1989.

(parties open to all without invitation), and banning the use of alcohol during rush.

According to the Simmons Market Research Bureau, consumption of beer, long the most popular alcoholic beverage among young people, is falling. In 1984, 56.3 percent of young people between the ages of 18 and 24 surveyed said they drank beer; by 1989, that percentage had fallen to 46 percent. In contrast, consumption of beer during that same time period fell only 1.6 percent among the population at large. [5]

By the same token, the tenth national survey by the University of Michigan's Institute for Social Research, conducted in 1989, [6], found positive changes in the attitudes of high school students toward drinking. In 1979, only 20.3 percent of students surveyed felt that moderate drinking (1 or 2 drinks almost every day) posed a "great" physical or mental risk. By 1988, however, 28.5 percent were aware of the dangers of so-called moderate drinking. The same survey disclosed that the percentage of high school seniors who said they had drunk an alcoholic beverage in the previous 30 days fell from approximately 72 percent in 1979 to about 60 percent in 1989.

Another encouraging sign in the struggle against alcohol abuse among the nation's teenagers can be found in the proliferation of alcohol-free prom and graduation parties across the country. These events, sponsored by community organizations and students themselves, began mostly in response to the tragedy of alcohol-related traffic injuries and deaths that haunt the aftermaths of high school and college galas. For example, in June 1989, the graduation ceremonies of a high school in New Jersey were capped off with a supervised all-night party at which drugs and alcohol were banned. The *New York Times* noted in its coverage of the event, "Such parties are intended to keep the graduates from drinking, and in many cases to keep them out of their cars, on what could be a big night for accidents." [7]

According to Steven D. Petterson, who works on programs to combat drug and alcohol abuse for the New York State Department of Education, "Getting seniors interested in such parties is sometimes difficult. But as the parties get more popular, the peer pressure to go gets harder." [8]

According to the same University of Michigan survey mentioned earlier, alcohol continues to be the drug of choice on college campuses. Although alcohol use has declined somewhat during the 1980s, it has not fallen nearly as far as use of other drugs. Unfortunately, the survey revealed that the drop in heavy drinking–students who had drunk 5 or more drinks in a row sometime within the 2 weeks preceding the survey—between 1985 and 1989 was statistically insignificant. The number of students who said they had drunk daily during the previous 30 days dropped to 4 percent from a high of 7 percent in 1984. And 9 out of 10 students said they had had one drink or more in the last 12 months, a percentage that has remained virtually unchanged throughout the 1980s. [9]

On the brighter side, though, there does seem to be a new caution and restraint among "moderate" college drinkers. According to William Bailey, the director of the alcohol-drug information center at Indiana University at Bloomington, "There is some indication that those who fall in the occasional drinking pattern are drinking less frequently and drinking less per occasion. There is not too much indication that heavy binge drinking has changed." He continues, "There is little change in what we call the annual prevalence of drinking. What has changed—and I am not sure this is related to the drinking laws—is that some institutions are reporting significant downward turns in some of the problems associated with alcohol consumption." [10] Reflecting on the survey's findings, Ruth Engs, associate professor of applied health sciences at Indiana University, who has studied college drinking patterns since 1974, noted, "The decrease in the percentage of students drinking came from those light to moderate drinkers and not from the heavier drinkers." [11]

READING THE SIGNS

Clearly, society has marshaled many resources to defend itself against the menace of alcoholism. The social welfare system has mechanisms in place for prevention, intervention, and treatment. There is reason to believe that alcohol education programs and changes in public attitudes toward drinking are creating social alternatives to excessive drinking among young people. A proliferation of treatment options is available to the alcoholic who recognizes that he or she has a problem and seeks help.

But with the best will in the world, outside agencies can only do so much. Finally, it is up to each individual to decide, if he or she drinks at all, to do so responsibly. Unless full-blown alcoholism has been established, it is possible for those who drink to excess to moderate their drinking. In fact, this is exactly what happened in many cases as laws against alcohol-impaired driving began to stiffen. People realized, sometimes to their own aston-

Did You Know That . . .

The cost for treatment for alcoholism and all alcohol-related disorders in the United States is more than 15 percent of the entire national health-care cost.

ishment, that it is possible to enjoy a social occasion without relying on alcohol; "designated drivers" stayed sober throughout the evening and provided rides home for others in their party who were free to indulge. In reaction to the excesses of the late 1960s and early 1970s, a "new temperance" took hold during the 1980s; sales of hard liquor plummeted, and consumption of wine coolers, light beers, and mineral water soared. When forced to examine their drinking habits in light of a new public awareness of the dangers of alcohol and other drug use in general, many Americans made the wise choice and decided to moderate their drinking.

Getting Help: What to Consider

Selecting an alcoholism treatment program isn't easy. The following guidelines were compiled by Herbert W. Winstead, chief of the Alcoholism Program of the Montgomery County (Md.) Health Department, and Christine Lubinski, Washington, D.C. representative of the National Council on Alcoholism.

1. *Cost.* How much is the program, and will my insurance cover it? If my insurance covers it partly, how much must I pay out of pocket? Can I pay over a period of time? Are there any costs tacked on after formal treatment, such as for "aftercare" or subsequent therapy group sessions?
2. *Certification.* Is your program certified by the state or any other agency, such as the Joint Commission on Accreditation of Hospitals (JCAH)? This is a must.
3. *Goals.* What are your treatment goals? Abstinence—not controlled drinking or the ability to drink socially—is key.
4. *Time.* How long is your program, and does it include detoxification? Do you ever extend the time period?
5. *Alcoholics Anonymous.* Do you make AA an integral part of your treatment plan? This is important for long-term recovery.
6. *Aftercare.* Do you have an aftercare program? How long? Experts consider 12 weeks of aftercare, including counseling, to be minimum.
7. *Family.* What do you do for the family of a client? Experts say the family should be involved in the entrance interview, in groups during treatment and in Al-Anon, AA's family support system.
8. *Staff.* What are the credentials of your staff? Experts say a medical doctor (M.D.) should be available at all times and counselors should be certified by the state. Winstead likes counselors to be an equal mix of recovered alcoholics and nonalcoholics.
9. *Philosophy.* Do you treat alcoholism as a physical disease, or as a symptom of an underlying cause or causes? If the latter is the

treatment approach, move on to another center, Winstead and Lubinski agree.

10. *Recovery rate.* What is your recovery rate, based on how long a follow-up sample? The average, Winstead says, is 75 to 80 percent, based on one- and two-year follow-ups.

11. *Medications.* Do you prescribe mood-changing drugs beyond the detoxification stage? Under what circumstances? If the answer is yes, Lubinski says, get another opinion.

12. *Treatment plan.* Is an individual treatment plan devised for each patient?

13. *Services for women.* Are there any special services if the client is female? In coed therapy, for instance, there may be two or three females to 20 or 25 males, many of them with a history of, say, abuse of women. Women-only therapy groups should be a part of the treatment.

Source: Robert H. Wilson, "Treatment of Alcoholism," *Consumers' Research* (December 1985), p. 18.

It goes without saying that most alcoholics and potential alcoholics cannot solve their drinking problems alone. Still, even the barest start on the road to recovery requires that someone with a drinking problem admit that he or she is in trouble and willing to go to any lengths to get better.

There are early warning signs of alcohol dependence, and anyone who exhibits them should sit down with a knowledgeable counselor and work out the treatment program that best suits his or her individual case. Here is a partial check list of indications that alcohol use is veering out of control. Remember, rigorous self-honesty is crucial to developing an accurate profile of one's own drinking patterns.

Someone has a serious drinking problem if he or she:

- Suffers anxiety and remorse "the morning after"
- Gradually increases alcoholic intake and becomes intoxicated more frequently
- Is interested in drinking for its own sake and may often drink alone
- Attempts to conceal drinking; sneaks drinks at parties; has two drinks in the kitchen for every round served in the living room; drinks before and/or after the party
- Refuses to admit drinking to excess and is annoyed when references are made to his or her drinking habits
- Pays less attention to personal appearance and hygiene or is

overly preoccupied with "covering up" the visible signs of a hangover

- Has guilt feelings that induce excuses for drinking behaviors
- Misses work because of over-indulgence
- Appears to be less stable, changes jobs frequently, or accepts work below his or her ability level
- Finds family differences and discord becoming intensified with increased intake
- Is arrested for public drunkenness or operating a vehicle while alcohol-impaired

According to the newly revised *Diagnostic and Statistical Manual of Mental Disorders,* signs of more advanced dependency include:

- Drinking more or over a longer period of time than had been intended
- A persistent desire or one or more unsuccessful attempts to cut down or control alcohol use
- Spending a great deal of time in activities necessary to obtain alcohol, drinking, and recovering from drinking
- Frequent intoxication or withdrawal symptoms when expected to fulfill major role obligations at work or home
- Giving up or reducing important social, occupational, or recreational activities because of alcohol abuse
- Continued drinking despite knowledge of having a problem that is caused or exacerbated by the use of the substance
- Marked tolerance; user needs at least a 50 percent increase over time in order to achieve intoxication or desired effect
- User shows withdrawal symptoms when drinking stops
- User drinks to avoid or relieve withdrawal symptoms

Taking an individual's entire personal history into account, a trained professional can diagnose a user's dependency as "mild," "moderate," or "severe" based on the above symptoms. Three are required for a diagnosis of **clinical dependency**, but the presence of just one could indicate that a user is in dependency's early stages and should get help. [12]

BEGIN WITHIN

Clinical dependency: A professional diagnosis of addiction to alcohol or other addictive substance.

The importance of early intervention in addictions of all kinds cannot be overstated. Alcoholics Anonymous (AA) reports that more and more people are seeking help before they have hit the

(continued on p. 120)

Do You Have a Drinking Problem? A Self-Test

The questions which follow have been culled from a variety of such questionnaires and categorized for easy reference. Some treatment programs will say that a "yes" answer to three or more of these questions is indicative of an alcoholism diagnosis.

We offer no such numerical standards, but if you are concerned about your drinking, or the drinking of a friend or loved one, check this out.

The more "yes" answers there are, the more the chances are that a person is a problem drinker or alcoholic, and in need of help.

1. HOW MUCH DO YOU DRINK?

- ☐ Do you drink more now than in the past?
- ☐ Do your friends drink less than you do?
- ☐ Do you drink until the bottle is empty?

2. HOW IMPORTANT IS DRINKING TO YOU?

- ☐ Do you avoid social functions where alcohol is not available?
- ☐ Do you insist on going to restaurants where alcohol is served?
- ☐ Do you look forward to occasions which permit drinking?
- ☐ Do you hang out with a crowd who drinks?
- ☐ Are most of your friends heavy drinkers?
- ☐ Do you ever hide a bottle to be sure you won't run out?

3. CONTROL

- ☐ Do you ever drink in the morning?
- ☐ Are there times when you find it necessary to completely avoid alcohol, to go on the wagon?
- ☐ Is it ever a struggle for you to stop drinking after 1 or 2 drinks?
- ☐ Are you unable to stop drinking whenever you want to?
- ☐ Have you broken promises to stop drinking?
- ☐ Do you ever gulp your drinks?

4. GENETIC, FAMILY

- ☐ Have your parents ever had trouble with alcohol?
- ☐ Do any of your brothers or sisters have trouble with alcohol?
- ☐ Any of your children have trouble with alcohol?

5. WHY DO YOU DRINK?

- ☐ Do you drink to build up your self confidence?
- ☐ Do you drink because you are shy?
- ☐ Do you drink before a date?
- ☐ Do you get along better, generally, when you drink?
- ☐ Do you drink to escape from worries and responsibilities?
- ☐ Does drinking give you a sense of power?

6. HOW DO YOU FEEL ABOUT YOUR DRINKING?

- ☐ Do you have a low self image, self esteem?
- ☐ Feel guilty about your drinking?
- ☐ Do you think you may have a drinking problem?
- ☐ Ever feel a need to cut down on your drinking?
- ☐ Does your drinking affect your reputation, and if so, do you care?

7. HOW DO OTHER PEOPLE FEEL ABOUT YOUR DRINKING?

- ☐ Do other people worry about your drinking?
- ☐ Are others embarrassed about your drinking?
- ☐ Do others have to lie about your drinking?
- ☐ Do others have to make excuses about your drinking, such as to your employer?
- ☐ Has anyone ever talked to you about your drinking?
- ☐ Are your children afraid of you when you have been drinking?
- ☐ Do your friends and relatives think you are a normal drinker?
- ☐ Have you ever lost friends because of your drinking?
- ☐ Has anyone ever sought help for you because of your drinking?

- ☐ Do your friends and family feel unpleasant around the holidays because of your drinking?

8. DENIAL

- ☐ Do you refuse to discuss whether you may have a problem with your drinking?
- ☐ Do you turn off to lectures or discussions about drinking problems?
- ☐ Do you make excuses for your drinking behavior?
- ☐ Do you lie about your drinking, try to cover it up?
- ☐ Do you break promises to stop drinking?
- ☐ Do you deny there is a problem, because you drink only beer?

9. BEHAVIOR

- ☐ Does your behavior change? For example, if you are normally mild-mannered, do you become aggressive when drinking?
- ☐ Do you ever get in fights when you have been drinking?
- ☐ Have you ever had a complete lapse of memory from drinking?
- ☐ Ever forgotten or denied things which have happened when you were drinking?
- ☐ Ever awake the morning after drinking and not remember a part or all of what happened the night before?

10. MEDICAL PROBLEMS

- ☐ Severe shaking?
- ☐ Hear voices?
- ☐ Problems with liver, cirrhosis?
- ☐ Doctor ever told you to cut down or stop drinking?
- ☐ Ever been to a hospital because of your drinking?

11. DRINKING INTERFERING WITH OTHER PARTS OF YOUR LIFE

- ☐ Ever arrested for drunk or impaired driving?
- ☐ Ever arrested for disorderly conduct or other alcohol-related offense?
- ☐ Ever had financial difficulties because of your drinking?
- ☐ Ever had family problems because of your drinking?
- ☐ Ever lost work because of drinking?
- ☐ Ever lost school because of drinking?

Source: Robert L. Hammond, *Almost All You Ever Wanted to Know About Alcoholism, and a Few Things You May Not Want to Know* (Lansing, MI: Alcohol Research Information Service, 1986), pp.10–12.

kind of rock bottom that involves loss of job, family, and home; an increasing number of people still in their teenage years and early twenties are entering treatment facilities and going on to become fully participating members of AA.

Used sensibly, alcohol is a relatively harmless potion. Used to avoid life's conflicts, risks, and responsibilities, however, it is a drug every bit as ruinous as heroin or cocaine. Only the individual can characterize his or her own relationship with alcohol and, if need be, summon the courage to change.

Glossary

A

Acetaldehyde: A colorless water-soluble liquid produced by the partial breakdown (oxidation) of ethanol, the active ingredient in alcoholic beverages; volatile and flammable (if exposed to air), it is also toxic.

Acetate: A by-product (metabolite) of the body's breakdown of alcohol. It is chemically related to acetic acid.

Acetylcholine: A neurotransmitter involved in the activation of muscle movement, memory, motivation, and arousal.

Adaptive-stage alcoholism: The first stage of chronic alcoholism, during which the drinker is able to function normally despite his or her drinking problem.

Addiction: A chronic, compulsive, or uncontrollable craving for and dependence on a particular substance or activity.

Alcohol dehydrogenase (ADH): An enzyme naturally present throughout the body that helps metabolize alcohol, primarily in the liver and stomach.

Alcoholic cardiomyopathy: A degenerative heart condition caused by excessive alcohol consumption.

Alcoholic hepatitis: An inflammation of the liver caused by excessive alcohol consumption; symptoms include lethargy, nausea, fever, and jaundice.

Alcoholic myopathy: A degenerative muscle disorder associated with chronic alcoholism.

Alcoholics Anonymous (AA): A voluntary organization founded in 1935, consisting of individuals seeking help for a drinking problem. The AA program is based on total abstinence, achieved by following a 12-step process.

Alcoholism: A disorder characterized by habitual and excessive drinking of alcoholic beverages. It impairs daily social functioning, job performance, and physical health.

Anemia: A blood disorder characterized by a decrease in the number of red blood cells or in the amount of hemoglobin they contain; symptoms include fatigue, weakness, and pallor.

Anxiety: An emotional state characterized by general uneasiness, apprehension, or fear.

Arrhythmia: Irregular heartbeat.

Atrophy: A wasting away of bodily tissues.

Axon: A tail-like filament that projects from the body of a nerve cell (neuron) along which nerve impulses (signals) are conducted between the nerve cell and other neurons or tissue.

B

Bacchanalia: Feasts celebrating Bacchus, the Roman god of wine.

Behavior modification: A type of therapy based upon the system of reward and punishment for specific actions.

Bile: A yellow or greenish liquid secreted by the liver, stored in the gallbladder, and released into the small intestine. It plays a major role in the metabolism of fats and the activation of other digestive enzymes.

Blood alcohol concentration (BAC): The percentage of alcohol found in the bloodstream; it is used to determine levels of intoxication.

Bootlegger: A person smuggling liquor from foreign countries or selling it illegally in the United States.

C

Cell: The basic structural unit of living organisms, consisting of an exterior wall or membrane, a nucleus, cytoplasm, and other structures.

Central nervous system: The brain and spinal cord.

Cerebellum: The part of the brain responsible for muscle and movement control, and coordination of eye and body movement.

Cerebral cortex: The part of the brain in which thought and memory processes take place.

Chronic alcoholism: Alcoholism that persists over an extended period of time.

Chronic obstructive lung diseases (COLD): The current label for a class of respiratory infections, ranging from chronic but usually harmless disorders such as bronchitis to potentially fatal illnesses such as emphysema.

Cirrhosis: A degenerative disease of the liver characterized by the accumulation of large fatty deposits and scar tissue that impairs functioning; the major causes of cirrhosis are chronic liver inflammation, hepatitis B, and chronic alcoholism.

Clinical dependency: A professional diagnosis of addiction to alcohol or other addictive substance.

Cognitive: Pertaining to thought and memory.

Computerized tomography (CT): A technology that makes it possible to generate highly detailed cross-sectional images of the body; also known as computerized axial tomography (CAT).

Confabulation: Fabrication invented by an alcoholic who can't remember actual events.

Congestive heart failure: A chronic disease of the heart characterized by greatly reduced pumping efficiency, accompanied by enlargement of the heart muscle and the buildup of fluid throughout the body.

Convulsions: Bodily contortions caused by violent involuntary muscle contractions, sometimes accompanied by loss of consciousness.

Correlational studies: Studies in which the researcher attempts to measure the extent to which one or more variables or characteristics are associated (correlated) with one or more other variables or characteristics.

Cytoplasm: A jelly-like substance found in all plant and animal cells that is contained by the cells's external layer (membrane), and within which the cell nucleus is suspended.

D

Delirium tremens (DTs): A psychotic reaction associated with chronic abuse of alcohol; symptoms include disorientation, hallucinations, intense fear, tremors, sweating, and fever.

Delta alcoholism: Alcoholism characterized by an inability to abstain from drinking.

Dendrites: Any of the branching protoplasmic structures of a nerve cell that receive impulses from other nearby cells.

Dependence: Reliance, either physical or psychological, on a psychoactive substance.

Depression: A mental state characterized by extreme sadness or dejection, both far out of proportion to the reality of the situation over which the sufferer is depressed.

Detoxification: The process of removing all traces of a poisonous substance from the body; also used to describe the initial phase of alcoholism or substance abuse treatment.

Diffusion: A process through which the molecules of one substance intermingle with the molecules of another substance.

Disease theory of alcoholism: A theory of alcoholism endorsed by Alcoholics Anonymous and others, in which alcoholism is seen as a disease rather than a character defect or social failing.

Distillation: A process in which liquids are heated to the boiling point to convert them to a gaseous state, after which the resulting vapors are cooled (condensed), making it possible to collect certain components of the original liquid, e.g., alcohol, in more concentrated form.

Distilled spirits: "Hard" liquor; beverages concocted through distillation, a process that consists of converting a liquid mixture into a vapor by heating it, then collecting the components by condensation.

Driving While Intoxicated (DWI): Operating a motor vehicle while under the influence of alcohol or other intoxicating drug.

E

Edema: An abnormal accumulation of fluid in the body.

Employee assistance programs (EAP): Counseling programs provided as a fringe benefit to employees by their employers; such programs come in a variety of forms and offer services ranging from substance abuse counseling to long-term therapy.

Endorphin: Any one of a related group of substances with a chemical structure similar to morphine. Endorphins are produced by the body (particularly by the nervous system) and relieve pain.

End-stage alcoholism: The final stage of chronic alcoholism, in which the drinker is usually socially and emotionally isolated and his or her physical health (and life) is at risk.

Enzyme: A protein that can cause chemical changes in other substances without being changed itself.

Epithelium: One or more of the cellular layers that completely cover the surface of the body, including the interior cavities and passages.

Esophagus: A muscular tube situated between the larynx and stomach; it is essential to digestion.

Ethanol: The colorless, volatile form of alcohol that is the active ingredient in alcoholic beverages; also known as ethyl alcohol or grain alcohol.

Etiology: The scientific cause of a disease; also the study of the causes of disease generally.

F

Felony: A major criminal offense, especially one punishable by substantial fine or imprisonment.

Fermentation: The process by which the sugar and starches present in fruits or other foods are converted into alcohol.

Fetal alcohol syndrome (FAS): A pattern of birth defects, cardiac abnormalities, and developmental retardation seen in babies of alcoholic mothers or mothers who abuse alcohol during pregnancy.

Fetus: A developing child from the eighth week of pregnancy to birth.

G

Gamma alcoholism: Alcoholism characterized by an inability to stop drinking once consumption of alcohol has started.

Gamma-aminobutyric acid (GABA): A neurotransmitter that scientists believe regulates anxiety in the brain.

Gateway drugs: A label applied to legal (licit) drugs such as alcohol, nicotine, and caffeine that are thought to serve as "gateways" to the use of other intoxicating substances, especially the so-called hard drugs.

Genetically: Pertaining to heredity; of or involving genes.

Glia: Cells in the central nervous system that regulate the chemical environment of the nerve cells. RNA is stored in glial cells.

Glycogen: A form of complex carbohydrate stored in the body. It is found primarily in liver and muscle tissue.

H

Halfway houses: Residential treatment facilities for alcoholism and other disorders, where patients are allowed to participate in outside activities while in treatment.

Hallucinations: Sensory perceptions not based on reality.

Hemorrhage: Uncontrollable, excessive bleeding.

Hippocampus: One of several structures in the central part of the brain that comprise the limbic system; the hippocampus plays an important role in memory processing.

Hormone: Any of the chemical substances secreted by glands in the body that are released directly into the bloodstream and elicit specific responses from a targeted organ, muscle, or other structure.

Hyperactivity: A pattern of excessive activity, easy distractibility, and impulsiveness accompanied by a short attention span; it appears in early life and is more common in boys than in girls.

Hypertension: The medical term for abnormally high blood pressure.

I

Inpatient programs: Alcohol treatment programs usually offered at clinics or hospitals, which require the patient to remain on the premises for a given period of time.

Intervention: A procedure in which friends or members of a substance abuser's family, usually working with the assistance of a professional therapist, directly confront the abuser at a prearranged time and place in an attempt to persuade him or her to seek immediate treatment.

Intoxication: A state in which one's ability to function is clearly and significantly impaired as a result of the consumption of alcohol or other intoxicating substance.

J

Jaundice: A yellow discoloring of the skin and eyes caused by the deposition of bile pigments.

K

Korsakoff's syndrome: A particularly dramatic form of amnesia associated with chronic alcohol abuse in which the individual is unable to recall virtually any of his or her recent or remote past; victims often attempt to cope by "recalling" events that never happened (confabulating).

L

Larynx: The upper part of the trachea; it contains the vocal cords.

Latchkey children: Term used to describe young children who are left alone for all or a substantial portion of the day, especially children whose parent or parents work outside the home.

Lesions: Localized, abnormal structural changes in any part of the body.

Life-style: A style of living that consistently reflects a particular set of values and attitudes.

Limbic system: A set of structures in the brain that influences motivation and emotional behavior.

Lipoproteins: A class of proteins found in the blood that consist of a simple protein combined with a lipid (fatty substances that are otherwise insoluble in water). They are transported throughout the body by the blood, and are one of the body's important sources of food energy.

Liver: A soft, reddish-brown organ that is the largest gland in the body; its many important functions include the destruction of red blood cells, the regulation of carbohydrate metabolism, and the detoxification of drugs and other substances, including alcohol.

M

Malignant melanoma: A highly malignant skin cancer originating in the pigment-secreting cells in the skin.

Malnutrition: An inadequate or unbalanced consumption of nutrients that produces negative effects on physical health.

Medulla oblongata: A structure within the brain stem that helps regulate basic bodily functions such as breathing and heart rate.

Menopause: The period during which a woman's menstrual cycle ceases for normal reasons; the "change of life."

Metabolic adaptation: Any adjustment in the body's normal metabolic processes undertaken in response to a persistent or long-standing abnormal condition.

Metabolism: The physical and chemical process whereby the body transforms food into energy by breaking large molecules into smaller molecules.

Metabolite: Any chemical by-product of the metabolic process.

Middle-stage alcoholism: The second stage of chronic alcoholism, during which the drinker's body develops a tolerance for alcohol that requires the consumption of increasingly greater quantities to avoid the onset of withdrawal symptoms.

Mitochondria: Small bodies, or organelles, found in living cells. They contain the enzymes used in metabolism; mitochondria are the "powerhouses" of the cell.

Molecule: The smallest unit of a substance that exhibits all of the substance's properties and is capable of independent existence; molecules ordinarily consist of 2 or more atoms joined together.

Morphine: An opium derivative, sometimes used as a pain reliever, that produces a sense of euphoria in the user; prolonged use can lead to both physical and psychological dependence.

Mothers Against Drunk Driving (MADD): A voluntary group founded in 1980 that provides support to victims of drunk drivers and their families and lobbies for tougher policies to curb drunk driving.

N

Narcissism: A preoccupation with and love of one's self and one's own physical or mental attributes.

Nasopharynx: The upper part of the oral cavity; it connects to the nasal passages.

Neurons: Impulse-conducting cells that are the functioning units of the nervous system.

Neurotransmitters: The chemical messengers that convey messages from one neuron to another.

Nucleus: A sac-like structure found in all living cells that contains the cell's genetic material.

O

Obsessive-compulsive behavior: Behavior in which the individual seeks to control recurrent and persistent anxiety-evoking thoughts by repetitive actions.

Outpatient programs: Alcohol treatment programs that allow the patient to live at home during the rehabilitation process.

P

Pancreas: A soft, triangular-shaped gland that secretes a variety of digestive enzymes, including insulin, which regulates the body's metabolism of sugar.
Paranoia: A form of schizophrenia characterized by delusions of grandeur and a suspicion of others, particularly a strong belief that one or more other individuals are out to "get" the sufferer.
Physiologically: Pertaining to bodily functions.
Placenta: The organ that develops in a woman's uterus during pregnancy and supplies the fetus with nourishment before its birth.
Postpartum depression: A depressed state experienced by some mothers shortly after the birth of a child.
Prohibition: The U.S. Constitution's Eighteenth Amendment, enacted in 1919 and repealed in 1932; it outlawed the sale of liquor in the United States.
Prothrombin: A protein found in the blood plasma that, when activated, is converted to thrombin, which in turn plays a major role in blood coagulation (clotting).
Psychoactive: Having the potential to alter mood or behavior.
Psychological: Relating to the mind.
Psychosis: A severe form of mental illness characterized by a deranged personality, delusions, or hallucinations.

R

Receptor: A specific molecule in a neural cell that receives messages from a neighboring neuron.
Rehabilitation: The process of recovering from a disease such as alcoholism.
Reticular activating system: Scattered groups of nerve cells located in the brain stem that collectively screen and regulate the flow of sensory information to the brain; also known as the reticular formation.

S

Self-help: Label applied to treatment programs in which lay people rather than professionals are the primary source of assistance and support.
Serotonin: A neurotransmitter, produced in the brain stem, that is involved in sleep and sensory experiences.
Somatostatin-14: A neurotransmitter, produced in the brain and pancreas, that helps regulate the production of insulin.
Spinal cord: A tubular cord of nerve tissue that is surrounded by the vertebrae and serves as the primary channel for sensory and motor messages between the brain and the rest of the body.
Sputum: A mixture of saliva combined with mucous and other substances secreted by the lining of the respiratory tract.
Stress: Any outside influence or event that produces a demand on the individual to adjust; stress may be either positive or negative.
Student assistance programs (SAP): Counseling programs provided by schools and other educational institutions to their students; as with employee assistance programs, the services offered vary from program to program.
Students Against Driving Drunk (SADD): A student group founded in the early 1980s to educate young people about the dangers of driving drunk.
Sulci: Valleys or fissures on the surface of the brain.
Synapse: The juncture between neurons.

T

Temperance: Moderation; temperance movements in the United States stressed moderation, or even total abstinence from alcohol.
Therapist: An individual who is trained in the treatment of one or more types of mental or physical disorder.
Thiamine (B_1): A B-complex vitamin found in green vegetables and other foods that is essential to the proper functioning of the nervous, digestive, and circulatory systems.
Tippler: Colloquial term used to describe one who drinks intoxicating beverages, especially to excess.
Tolerance: The gradual desensitization of the body to the effects of alcohol.
Toper: A 17th-century term used to describe a heavy drinker.
Tranquilizers: Any of a variety of prescription drugs that depress the central nervous system,

thus relieving anxiety and tension and sometimes relaxing the muscles.

Triglycerides: Fatty compounds found in foods and made in the body, consisting of a carbon "backbone" to which are attached three fatty acids.

12 Steps: A generic label used to describe the 12 basic steps that serve as guidelines for the Alcoholics Anonymous treatment program, or similar guidelines used by other self-help groups.

V

Varices: Abnormally dilated and misshapen blood vessels; plural of varix.

Ventricles: Fluid-filled cavities in the center of the brain.

Volstead Act: The congressional act that outlined the policies for Prohibition.

W

Wernicke's syndrome: A condition characterized by paralysis of normal eye movements, problems with walking, and disordered thinking.

Withdrawal: The process the body goes through if denied a substance upon which it has become dependent.

Notes

CHAPTER 1

1. *Drinking: Alcohol in American Society–Issues and Current Research,* John A. Ewing and Beatrice A. Rouse, eds. (Chicago: Nelson-Hall, 1979), 6.
2. A. Lichine, *Encyclopedia of Wines and Spirits* (New York: Alfred A. Knopf, 1968), 1.
3. Ewing and Rouse, p. 11.
4. S. P. Lucia, *Alcohol and Civilization* (New York: McGraw-Hill, 1960), 129–130.
5. Ewing and Rouse, p. 43.
6. J. R. Gusfield, *Symbolic Crusade: Status Politics and the American Temperance Movement* (Champaign: University of Illinois Press, 1963).
7. Thomas Babor, *Alcohol: Customs and Rituals* (New York: Chelsea House Publishers, 1986), 49.
8. E. H. Cherrington, *The Evolution of Prohibition in America* (Boston, MA: American Issue Press, 1920), 78.
9. Ewing and Rouse, p. 45.
10. Jean McBee Knox, *Drugs Through the Ages* (New York: Chelsea House Publishers, 1986), 64.
11. Ewing and Rouse, p. 5.
12. E. M. Jellinek, "Recent Trends in Alcoholism and in Alcohol Consumption," *Quarterly Journal of Studies on Alcohol* 7 (1948): 1–42.
13. H. Asbury, *The Great Illusion* (Westport, CT: Greenwood Publishing Group, 1950), 13.
14. George C. Vaillant, "Is Alcoholism a Unitary Disorder?" *The Natural History of Alcoholism: Causes, Patterns, and Paths to Recovery* (Cambridge, MA: Harvard University Press, 1983).

CHAPTER 2

1. Geraldine Youcha, *Women and Alcohol* (New York: Crown Publishing Group, a division of Random House, 1978), 62.
2. "Understanding Alcoholism," *Blue Print for Health,* Blue Cross and Blue Shield Association, XXVI, #1 (1984), 5–6, and William J. Bailey, *Drug Use in American Society: An Epidemiologic Analysis of Risks* 2d Edition (Edina, MN: Burgess International Group, Bellwether Press Division, 1988), 165.

3. James R. Milam and Katherine Ketcham, *Under the Influence* (New York: Bantam Books, 1981), 19–20.
4. Youcha, p. 118.
5. Mario Frezza, M.D., et al., "High Blood Alcohol Levels in Women," *New England Journal of Medicine* 322, no. 2 (11 January 1990): 95–99, 127–129.
6. Frezza et al., pp. 95–99, 127–129.
7. "Scientists Pinpoint Brain Irregularities in Drug Addicts," *New York Times*, 26 June 1990, C1, C4.
8. "Scientists Pinpoint Brain Irregularities in Drug Addicts," C4.
9. "Scientists Pinpoint Brain Irregularities in Drug Addicts," C4.
10. Jon Zonderman and Laurel Shader, M.D., *Drugs and Disease* (New York: Chelsea House Publishers, 1987), 44.
11. Ewing and Rouse, p. 20.

CHAPTER 3

1. *Seventh Special Report to the U.S. Congress on Alcohol and Health*, Department of Health and Human Services, Public Health Service, Alcohol, Drug Abuse, and Mental Health Administration, National Institute on Alcohol Abuse and Alcoholism, January 1990.
2. *Seventh Special Report on Alcohol and Health.*
3. *Seventh Special Report on Alcohol and Health.*
4. Milam and Ketcham, p. 9, and *Seventh Special Report on Alcohol and Health.*
5. *Alcohol and Women*, American College of Obstetricians and Gynecologists (Washington, DC: 1986).
6. *Alcohol and Women.*
7. *The Challenge* 4, no. 2 (November/December 1989): 4.
8. *The Challenge*, p. 4.
9. Jane Brody, "Personal Health," *New York Times*, 12 July 1988, B6.
10. Sara Nelson, "A Nation Under the Influence," *Seventeen*, March 1990, 183.
11. Robert S. Mendelsohn, *Confessions of a Medical Heretic* (Chicago, IL: Contemporary Books, 1979), 127.
12. *New York Times*, July 1986.
13. Peter Gwynne, *Who Uses Drugs?* (New York: Chelsea House Publishers, 1988), 43.
14. Gwynne, p. 43.
15. Jean Knox, *Drinking, Driving, and Drugs* (New York: Chelsea House Publishers, 1988), 66.

16. Knox.
17. Knox.
18. Knox.

CHAPTER 4

1. Ross Fishman, *Alcohol and Alcoholism* (New York: Chelsea House Publishers, 1987), 54.
2. Edward Edelson, *Drugs and the Brain* (New York: Chelsea House Publishers, 1987), 46.
3. Edelson, p. 47.
4. B. F. Grant, M. C. Dufour, and T. C. Hartford, "Epidemiology of Alcoholic Liver Disease," *Seminar on Liver Disease* 8, no. 1 (1988): 12–25.
5. *Seventh Annual Report on Alcohol and Health.*
6. R. Wang et al., "Alcohol and Dilated Cardiomyopathy: Incidence and Correlation with Clinical Outcome," *Journal of Substance Abuse Treatment* 4, nos. 3–4 (1987): 209–213.
7. J. Decker and J. Goldstein, "Risk Factors in Head and Neck Cancer," *New England Journal of Medicine* 306 (1982): 1151–1155, and H. E. Driver and P. F. Swan, "Alcohol and Human Cancer" (review), *Anticancer Research* 7 (1987): 309–320.
8. National Clearing House for Alcohol and Drug Information, *Fact Sheet*, June 1987.
9. Stanton Peele, "Second Thoughts About a Gene for Alcoholism," *Atlantic Monthly,* June 1990, 52–58.
10. Peele, pp. 52–58.
11. Peele, pp. 52–58.
12. Peele, pp. 52–58.
13. Peele, pp. 52–58.
14. Peele, pp. 52–58.
15. Milam and Ketcham.
16. Peele, pp. 52–58.
17. "Alcohol Use and Great Expectations," *Science News* 132, 3 October 1987, 218.
18. Peele, pp. 52–58.

CHAPTER 5

1. Thomas Trotter, "Essay, Medical, Philosophical, and Chemical on Drunkenness," in M. Mann, *Primer on Alcoholism* (Orlando: Holt, Rhinehart & Winston, 1950), 6.

2. Jean Kinney and Gwen Leaton, *Loosening the Grip, A Handbook of Alcohol Information,* (St. Louis: C. V. Mosby & Year Book Medical Publishers, 1978), 179.
3. Kinney and Leaton, p. 179.
4. Mary Ellen Pinkham, *How to Stop the One You Love From Drinking* (New York: G. P. Putnam's Sons, 1986), 296–320.
5. Kenneth H. Bacon, "Private Drug Abuse Treatment Centers Try to Adjust to Life in the Slow Lane," *Wall Street Journal*, 23 July 1990, B1.
6. Pinkham, pp. 296–320.
7. Bacon, p. B1.
8. Alcoholics Anonymous General Service Office, Public Information Office, New York, NY.
9. Alcoholics Anonymous General Service Office, Public Information Office, New York, NY.
10. *Alcoholics Anonymous* (Alcoholics Anonymous World Services, Inc., 1939), and *Twelve Steps and Twelve Traditions* (Alcoholics Anonymous World Services, Inc., 1953).
11. Fishman, 99–102.
12. Fishman.

CHAPTER 6

1. Jean Knox, *Drinking, Driving, and Drugs* (New York: Chelsea House Publishers, 1988), 68.
2. *New York Times*, 21 August 1990.
3. Department of Health and Human Services, Alcohol, Drug Abuse and Mental Health Administration, Office for Substance Abuse Prevention, *Prevention*, 14–15.
4. Maura Reynolds, "Student Drinking Creates Problems for Colleges," *New York Times*, 28 February 1988, A38.
5. Marj Charles, "Youthful Sobriety Tests Liquor Firms," *Wall Street Journal,* 14 June 1990.
6. "Monitoring the Future" (University of Michigan Institute for Social Research, 1989).
7. Sara Lyall, "Parties Keep Graduates Safe and Sober," *New York Times,* 28 June 1989, 25.
8. Lyall, p. 25.
9. Deirdre Carmody, "College Drinking: Changes in Attitude and Habit," *New York Times*, 7 March 1990, B5.
10. Carmody, p. B5.
11. Carmody, p. B5.
12. *Mademoiselle*, October 1987.

Resources

BOOKS

Alcoholics Anonymous: The Story of How Many Men and Women Have Recovered from Alcoholism. 3d ed. New York: Alcoholics Anonymous World Service, 1976.

This is the basic text, best known as the "Big Book," for Alcoholics Anonymous. Originally published in 1939, the third edition will be in its fortieth printing in 1991. The first third of the book has not changed since publication of the first edition. AA maintains that the nature of alcoholism does not require such change. The personal stories in the second two-thirds were updated and expanded in the third edition to represent more accurately the wide variety of individuals now finding recovery from alcoholism in AA. This edition has been approved by the General Service Conference of Alcoholics Anonymous. More than 4,000,000 copies have been printed since the first edition as testimony to how well the AA program works.

Basini, Richard A. *How To Cut Down Your Social Drinking.* New York: G. P. Putnam, 1985.

For people worried about drinking a bit too much, those who can't decide where they stand on the social drinking scale, or those who are annoyed with the extra pounds that social drinking adds, this book might be of value. Written by a reformed social drinker who found that his drinking was affecting his health and his work, Basini shows how to distinguish between the 4 basic drinking situations and thus avoid disaster, how to reduce social drinking, and how celebrities and corporate presidents survive the cocktail circuit. Basini reveals through his interviews that highly successful people drink very little alcohol and that these people have methods to avoid extra or unwanted drinks. He shows clearly that controlling social drinking is a giant step toward success.

Beattie, Melody. *Codependent No More: How to Stop Controlling Others and Start Caring for Yourself.* New York: Harper & Row, 1987.

This book is useful for people who have become so absorbed in other people's problems that they do not have time to identify or solve their own problems. The author covers many compulsive disorders in the text, including the grip that alcoholics have on family and friends. Codependents, by definition, are those people who are tormented by other people's compulsive behavior. Beattie details the characteristics of codependency, where the compulsive behavior comes from, and how it affects others. She discusses several options to controlling behavior for those who must deal with dependent personalities.

Gross, Leonard. *How Much is Too Much? The Effects of Social Drinking.* New York: Random House, 1983.

This book examines the effects social drinking has on the risk of illness and cognitive impairment. Gross sets out to define at which point drinking is no longer safe. Through intensive observations, surveys, measurements, and readings, the author reveals that most drinkers who think they drink moderately are not drinking moderately or safely at all. Gross also presents the links between alcohol and high blood pressure, the social drinker's increased risks of contracting cirrhosis of the liver and cancer, the chances for birth defects in the fetuses of expectant mothers who drink, how alcohol affects the brain, and the accuracy of those surveys indicating that 1 or 2 drinks a day might lead to better health and longer life.

Langone, John, and Dolores deNobrega Langone. *Women Who Drink.* Reading, MA: Addison-Wesley, 1980.

This book addresses the social, psychological, and physical factors that play a part in the drinking behavior of women. The authors attempt to answer questions about how women differ from men in their reasons for and patterns of drinking, how a woman responds to alcohol, what effects a woman's drinking has on her family and friends, and more. This information provides support to women who find themselves wondering about their drinking. The theme of the book is not abstinence from drinking, but responsible, careful alcohol use for those who choose to drink.

Ludwig, Arnold M. *Understanding the Alcoholic's Mind: The Nature of Craving and How to Control It.* New York: Oxford University Press, 1988.

The author believes that being sober is far more than simply not drinking; it is developing a new set of attitudes, values, and behaviors. To remain sober, alcoholics must recognize that powerful forces and dangerous frames of mind lure them back to alcohol. Ludwig presents his own research, the research of other experts, and several clinical examples and personal stories to show the basic principles necessary for achieving a successful recovery. The book is optimistic, showing that recovery is not an impossible task but an attainable goal for those who know what to do.

Luks, Allan, ed. *Having Been There: The Personal Drama of Alcoholism.* New York: Scribner's, 1979.

This book is a collection of 18 short stories. Selected from more than 500 entries in a national competition, the stories cover the entire range of alcoholism: from the beginning stages to habitual drunkenness, the difficult attempts to seek help, and finally the uncertain steps back to sobriety after giving up alcohol. These stories show that there are many different types of alcoholics and that the friends and relatives of alcoholics also suffer. Anyone interested in exploring personal thoughts and concerns about alcoholism will find this book valuable.

Mendelson, Jack H., and Nancy K. Mello. *Alcohol: Use and Abuse in America.* Boston: Little, Brown & Co., 1985.

The authors explore the use of alcohol from colonial times through the days of the Civil War, when alcohol was used in conjunction with opium and cocaine, to the time of Prohibition and the most recent efforts to regulate drinking. The book then examines how alcohol affects the brain, sex drive, and aggression, and how it provides the illusion of happiness. The health consequences of alcohol are examined as well as the effects of alcohol in combination with other drugs, such as medicines, hallucinogens, and marijuana. The authors show that alcoholism has complex causes and that there is no single underlying factor to influence alcoholism. Finally the authors present practical and compassionate information for alcoholism treatment, recovery, and prevention.

Robertson, Nan. *Getting Better: Inside Alcoholics Anonymous.* New York: William Morrow, 1988.

In this book Nan Robertson, Pulitzer Prize-winning reporter for the *New York Times,* tells the story of how two alcoholics, a surgeon and a failed stockbroker, helped each other stay sober and how their fellowship grew into today's worldwide organization. The author shows how AA works and why it succeeds. She introduces readers to the rehabilitation centers and explores the role religion plays in the AA program. Nan Robertson concludes with the story of her own battle with alcohol after the death of her husband and her eventual recovery through AA.

NEWSLETTERS

Harvard Health Letter is published monthly as a nonprofit service by the Department of Continuing Education, Harvard Medical School, in association with Harvard University Press. The letter attempts to interpret health information for general readers in a timely and accurate fashion. A one-year subscription is $21. Write to the Harvard Medical School Letter, 79 Garden Street, Cambridge, MA 02138, or call customer service at (617) 495-3975.

Healthline is published monthly by Healthline Publishing, Inc. The letter is intended to educate readers about ways to help themselves avoid illness and live longer, healthier lives. A one-year subscription is $19, or 2 years for $34. Write to Healthline, The C. V. Mosby Company, 11830 Westline Industrial Drive, St. Louis, MO 63146-3318, or call (800) 325-4177 (ext. 351).

Johns Hopkins Medical Letter, Health After 50 is published monthly by Medletter Associates, Inc., and covers a variety of topics related to healthful living. A one-year subscription is $20. Write to the Johns Hopkins Medical Letter, P.O. Box 420179, Palm Coast, FL 32142.

Lahey Clinic Health Letter is published monthly to bring readers timely, relevant information about important medical issues. Continuing topics include general healthfulness, natural and processed foods, depression, exercise, alcohol, prescription medicine therapy, major diseases, exercise, and more. A one-year subscription is $18. Write to the Lahey Clinic Health Letter, Subscription Department, P.O. Box 541, Burlington, MA 01805.

University of California Berkeley Wellness Letter is published monthly and covers many topics, including nutrition, fitness, and stress management. A one-year subscription is $20. Write to the University of California, Berkeley Wellness Letter, P.O. Box 420148, Palm Coast, FL 32142.

PERIODICALS

Al-Anon Family Group Headquarters—The Forum: A Meeting in My Pocket is published monthly by Al-Anon Family Group Headquarters and covers all topics related to alcoholism treatment, effects on family and friends, recovery, and other important information. Distributed internationally, the magazine is written by and for Al-Anon members. A one-year subscription costs $6. Write to Al-Anon Family Group, P.O. Box 862, Midtown Station, New York, NY 10018.

FDA Consumer is published 10 times a year by the Food and Drug Administration, U.S. Public Health Service, Department of Health and Human Services. This magazine provides about 6 feature articles on a wide range of topics related to health, health-care and health-care products, medicines, medical technologies, diseases, food safety, and so on. Regular columns include brief Updates; an AIDS Page; Investigator's Reports exposing frauds, public health concerns, and so on; and Summaries of Court Actions that provide information on drugs, medical services and devices, foods, and even veterinary drugs that have come under the scrutiny of the law. The subscription price is $12 a year. Write to FDA Consumer, Superintendent of Documents, Government Printing Office, Washington, DC 20402.

Health Magazine is published 10 times a year by Family Media, Inc. This magazine features 6 articles per issue on fitness for both mind and body, environmental topics, sporting activities, health, and food. It also has a regular Healthline section dealing with topics on behavior, medical information, and topics related to children's health. A one-year subscription is $19.95. Write to Health Magazine, Subscription Dept., P.O. Box 420030, Palm Coast, FL 32142-0030, or call (800) 423-1780; in Florida call (800) 858-0095.

In Health Magazine is published 6 times a year and provides articles on a number of health issues. In addition to recipes and practical nutrition tips, the magazine regularly includes self-help resources for consumers. A one-year subscription is $18. Write to In Health, P.O. Box 52431, Boulder, CO 80321-2431.

Priorities: For Long Life & Good Health is published quarterly by the American Council of Science and Health, Inc. (ACSH), a non-profit consumer education association promoting scientifically balanced evaluations of nutrition, chemicals, life-style factors, the environment, and human health. General individual membership in ACSH, which includes a subscription to *Priorities,* costs $25 a year. Write to the Subscription Department, Priorities, 1995 Broadway, 16th Floor, New York, NY 10023-5860

HOTLINES

Al-Anon Family Group Headquarters, (800) 356-9996. This organization of relatives and friends of persons with alcohol problems will answer questions from individuals about alcoholism and its effects, courses of treatment, and other relevant information.

National Council on Alcoholism, (800) NCA-CALL. This organization works to prevent and control alcoholism through programs of public and professional education, medical and scientific information, and public advocacy. Call for answers to questions on alcoholism and alcohol-related subjects and to receive pamphlets and other publications.

National Health Information Clearing House, Department of Health and Human Services, (800) 336-4797; in Maryland, call (301) 656-4167. Operated by the Office of Disease Prevention and Health Promotion, this information and referral center's trained personnel will direct callers to the organization or government agency that can assist with health questions, whether they are about high blood pressure, cancer, fitness, or any other topic. Available 9:00 A.M. to 5:00 P.M., Eastern Standard Time, Monday through Friday.

TARGET—Helping Students Cope With Alcohol and Drugs, (800) 464-5400. The TARGET Resource Center is a project of the National Federation of State High School Associations that provides information about helping students deal with drugs and alcohol. Call for resource information and referrals to literature, prevention programs, and treatment facilities for adolescents.

Tel-Med is a free telephone service provided in many cities. One can call, ask for a specific tape number, and have the health message played over the phone. There are over 300 medical topics to choose from, including topics related to maintaining a healthy life-style, and many states provide toll-free numbers for this service. Call your local information operator to find the nearest Tel-Med office or write to Tel-Med, Box 970, Colton, CA 92324.

VIDEOTAPES

FMS Productions offers a series of alcohol and drug abuse videos. For a complete list of titles and ordering information write FMS Productions, Inc., P.O. Box 4428, 520 East Montecito Street, Suite F, Santa Barbara, CA 93140, or call toll free (800) 421-4609.

GOVERNMENT, CONSUMER, AND ADVOCACY GROUPS

Al-Anon Family Group (AFG) Headquarters, P.O. Box 862, Midtown Station, New York, NY 10018, (212) 302-7240

Al-Anon is an organization for relatives and friends of persons with alcohol problems. Its membership includes Al-Ateen, a group for people 12 to 20 years of age whose lives have been adversely affected by someone with a drinking problem, most often a parent. Al-Anon publishes *Al-Anon Family Group Headquarters—The Forum: A Meeting in My Pocket* monthly. This is an international magazine written for and by Al-Anon members that includes a calendar of events. Al-Anon also publishes leaflets, pamphlets, and books.

Alcohol and Drug Problems Association (ADPA) of North America, 444 N. Capitol Street, NW, Suite 706, Washington, DC 20001, (202) 737-4340

Individuals and alcohol and drug agencies work together to study alcohol problems and drug abuse by exchange of information and to promote legislation and standards that contribute to the care and control of alcoholism. The organization maintains a continuing education program and a placement service; it also publishes a newsletter and book reviews.

Alcohol Research Information Service (ARIS), 1106 East Oakland, Lansing, MI 48906, (517) 485-9900

ARIS consists of individuals and corporations that collect, correlate, and disseminate information regarding alcohol and alcoholic products. The information is used to evaluate the effects of alcohol on the health and well-being of people in the United States. ARIS operates a clearinghouse for substance abuse information and provides pamphlets and teaching materials for elementary and secondary school levels. The organization maintains a library of 1000 volumes related to alcohol consumption and publishes *The Bottom Line* quarterly and *Monday Morning Report* semimonthly.

Alcoholics Anonymous (AA) World Service, P.O. Box 459, Grand Central Station, New York, NY 10163, (212) 686-1100

Founded in 1935, this international fellowship of women and men share their experiences, strength, and hope with each other so that they may solve their common problem and help others to recover from alcoholism and achieve sobriety. AA is not allied with any sect, denomination, political organization, or institution; it does not wish to engage in any controversy; and it neither endorses nor opposes any causes. AA is self-supported through membership contributions. The organization produces several publications designed to aid in the recovery from alcohol dependence.

Allied Youth and Family Counseling Center (AYFCC), 310 North Windmore, Dallas, TX 75208, (214) 943-1044

AYFCC provides an outpatient counseling program for youth and their families. The center's services include treatment for alcohol and drug abuse, marriage and family counseling, psychological testing, and insurance coverage. The center also sponsors an education program.

American Cancer Society (ACS), 1599 Cliffs Road, Atlanta, GA 30329, (404) 320-3333

The ACS supports education and research on the prevention, diagnosis, detection, and treatment of cancer, and the health effects of drinking in relation to cancer. The ACS provides special services to cancer patients and sponsors the support groups Reach to Recovery, CanSurmount, and I Can Cope.

American Council on Alcoholism (ACA), White Marsh Business Center, 5024 Campbell Boulevard, Suite H, Baltimore, MD 21236, (301) 529-9200

The ACA is a coalition of local, state, regional, and national groups working to end alcohol abuse and alcoholism. The ACA seeks to educate the public on issues concerning alcoholism and to promote employee assistance at the job site. The council maintains a 10,000-volume library of subjects related to the study of alcoholism and has a 24-hour telephone referral service for questions about alcoholism. The ACA publishes several periodicals and newsletters.

American Council of Science and Health (ACSH), 1995 Broadway, 16th Floor, New York, NY 10023, (212) 362-7044

The council's purpose is to provide consumers with scientifically balanced evaluations of food, chemicals, the environment, and human health. Council personnel participate in government regulatory proceedings, public debates, and other forums and write regularly for professional and scientific journals, popular magazines, and newspaper columns. The ACSH holds national press conferences and produces a self-syndicated series of health updates for radio. The council provides 24-hour computer on-line articles, commentaries, press releases, and questions and answers on health topics. It publishes brochures and pamphlets on numerous health topics as well as research reports on the health risks and benefits of various public health and environmental issues.

American Health and Temperance Society (AHTS), c/o Story Proctor, 6840 Eastern Avenue, NW, Washington, DC 20012, (202) 722-6736

The AHTS seeks to publicize, through popular education, the effects of alcohol, tobacco, and narcotics and to promote health by encouraging an alcohol- and drug-free way of life. The society sponsors competitions, bestows awards, conducts research programs, and offers children's services. The AHTS maintains a speakers' bureau and a 300-volume library. It publishes *Life and Health* and *Listen* monthly and *Winner* 9 times a year.

Americans for Substance Abuse Prevention and Treatment (ASAPT), 511 Capitol Court, NE, Number 300, Washington, DC 20002, (202) 347-7878

The organization seeks to increase public awareness through education concerning the warning signs of alcoholism and drug addiction. The group initiates and supports educational efforts directed toward the prevention of substance abuse, especially among youth. It participates in making policy, promotes legislation dealing with substance abuse, and encourages alcohol- and drug-related research. It also publishes several newsletters.

BACCHUS of The United States, National Headquarters, P.O. Box 10430, Denver, CO 80210, (303) 871-3068

BACCHUS is the acronym for Boost Alcohol Consciousness Concerning the Health of University Students; it is also the name of the Greek god of wine. Comprised of students, advisors, faculty, and staff of colleges and universities in the United States and Canada, the group's primary mission is to deliver alcohol education to college students and their communities. Through positive peer pressure, it promotes responsible decisions regarding the use of alcohol and discourages irresponsible or illegal use of alcohol. BACCHUS encourages alternative social activities, such as coffee houses, talent shows, and fun runs. The group produces several books and newsletters.

Children of Alcoholics Foundation (CAF), 200 Park Avenue, 31st Floor, New York, NY 10166, (212) 351-2680

The foundation seeks to educate the public about the children of alcoholics and stimulate interest in seeking solutions to their problems. It promotes research, educational and informational programs, and public discussion of alcoholism and its effects on children. The CAF disseminates reports and research results and publishes several newsletters.

Mothers Against Drunk Driving (MADD), 669 Airport Freeway, Suite 310, Hurst, TX 76053, (817) 268-6233

More than 1 million members comprise this group, which has 50 state and 400 local agencies. The organization encourages citizen participation in working toward reform of the drunk driving problem. It acts as the voice of victims of drunk driving crashes by speaking on their behalf to communities, businesses, and educational groups. MADD provides materials for use in medical facilities and health and driver education programs. MADD representatives serve on public, law enforcement, and legislative advisory boards and aid in establishing local, county, or state task forces. MADD provides victim assistance and supplies information for victims and their families about bereavement groups, the judicial system, and other assistance groups. The group publishes the *MADD National Newsletter* periodically, the quarterly *MADD in Action,* and several brochures.

National Council on Alcoholism (NCA), 12 West 21st Street, New York, NY 10010, (212) 206-6770

The council works for the prevention and control of alcoholism through programs of public and professional education, medical and scientific information, and public policy advocacy. It publishes pamphlets, books, and catalogs on aspects of alcoholism and its treatment.

National Listen America Club (NLAC), 2686 Townsgate Road, Westlake Village, CA 91359, (805) 497-9457

The club's members are junior and senior high-school students who have pledged not to smoke, drink alcohol, or use drugs for the purpose of "getting high." The club provides a variety of community service projects, including an annual national 2-hour television special. NLAC's projects are designed to recognize and promote the positive and constructive things young people are doing. The NLAC publishes *Listen America Magazine* monthly and *Tune In,* a biweekly newsletter.

The Other Victims of Alcoholism (TOVA), P.O. Box 921, Radio City Station, New York, NY 10101, (212) 247-8087

TOVA provides and disseminates to the public information and education about the less visible victims of alcoholism, from family members to industry. The group focuses on what it calls the "domino" effect of alcoholism and its impact on society. TOVA serves as an information clearinghouse and publishes *The Domino Quarterly* and numerous pamphlets, brochures, special reports, reprints, and other materials.

Students Against Driving Drunk (SADD), P.O. Box 800, Marlboro, MA 01752, (508) 481-3568

There are more than 50 state and 20,000 local SADD groups, which include both students and concerned adults. The objective of the organization is to increase public awareness of drunk driving and urge students to take action against it. SADD publishes several newsletters addressing students in colleges, high schools, junior high schools, and athletic programs. SADD also produces video- and audiocassettes.

TARGET–Helping Students Cope With Alcohol and Drugs, P.O. Box 20626, 11724 Plaza Circle, Kansas City, MO 64195, (816) 464-5400

TARGET is a project of the National Federation of State High School Associations that provides information about helping students deal with alcohol and drugs. TARGET acts as an information resource center on chemical abuse and its prevention. The group provides a referral service for publications and treatment facilities for adolescents from preschool through the 12th grade and publishes *On Target* 9 times a year as well as a brochure.

Women for Sobriety (WFS), P.O. Box 618, Quakertown, PA 18951, (212) 536-8026

Members include self-help groups of female alcoholics who use a 13-step program to reach a new way of thinking about themselves and thus remove the dependence on alcohol. The goal is complete abstinence from alcohol. The group recognizes the differences between male and female alcoholics and feels that understanding these differences is important for successful recovery. Small groups organize and meet independently. WFS publishes newsletters, books, booklets, and pamphlets.

Index

Page 6 From *The Alcoholic Republic: An American Tradition* by W. J. Rorabaugh. Copyright © 1979 by Oxford University Press, Inc. Reprinted by permission. Page 9 Reprinted with permission from *Journal of Studies on Alcohol,* vol. 37, pp. 360–361, 1976. Copyright © by Journal of Studies on Alcohol, Inc., Rutgers Center of Alcohol Studies, New Brunswick, N.J. 08903. Page 12 From *Alcohol: Use and Abuse in America* by Jack H. Mendelson, M. D., and Nancy K. Mello. Copyright © 1985 by Bio-Behavioral Research Corporation. Page 17 Reprinted with permission from John Langone. Page 28 Reprinted with permission from The Alcohol Research Information Service. Page 38 Copyright © 1985 by The New York Times Company. Reprinted by permission. Page 44 Reprinted from *Mayo Clinic Health Letter* with permission from the Mayo Foundation for Medical Education and Research. Page 46 Reprinted from *Better Homes and Gardens* magazine. Copyright © Meredith Corporation, 1988. Page 47 Copyright © 1988 by The New York Times Company. Reprinted by permission. Page 52 Reprinted with the permission of the Associated Press. Page 56 Reprinted with permission of Life Skills Education, 226 Libbey Parkway, Weymouth, MA 02189. Page 66 Excerpted from the October 1987 issue of the *Harvard Health Letter.* Copyright © 1987 by the President and Fellows of Harvard College. Page 69 Reprinted with permission from the American Council on Science and Health (ACSH), a nonprofit, consumer education institution located in New York. Page 73 Reprinted with permission from *Science News,* the weekly newsmagazine of science. Copyright © 1991 by Science Service, Inc. Page 84 Reprinted by permission from *Changing Times,* the Kiplinger Magazine, August 1984. Copyright © 1984 by The Kiplinger Washington Editors, Inc. Page 92 Copyright © by *U.S. News & World Report,* November 30, 1987. Page 98 Special reprint permission granted by *Current Health 2,* published by Field Publications. Copyright © 1990 by Field Publications. *Current Health* is a federally registered trademark of Field Publications. Page 103 Excerpted from the September 1990 issue of the *Harvard Health Letter.* Copyright © 1990 by the President and Fellows of Harvard College. Page 107 Copyright © 1984 by Time Warner Inc. Reprinted by permission. Page 116 Reprinted with permission from *Consumers' Research Magazine,* Washington, DC. Page 119 Reprinted with permission from the Alcohol Research Information Service.